AMERICAN GOVERNMENT

FROM THE
CONTINENTAL CONGRESS TO THE
IOWA CAUCUS, EVERYTHING YOU
NEED TO KNOW ABOUT **U.S. POLITICS**

101

KATHLEEN SEARS

Adams Media
New York London Toronto Sydney New Delhi

Adams Media
An Imprint of Simon & Schuster, Inc.
57 Littlefield Street
Avon, Massachusetts 02322

For information about special discounts for bulk purchases, please contact Simon & Schuster Special Sales at 1-866-506-1949 or business@simonandschuster.com.

The Simon & Schuster Speakers Bureau can bring authors to your live event. For more information or to book an event contact the Simon & Schuster Speakers Bureau at 1-866-248-3049 or visit our website at www.simonspeakers.com.

Manufactured in the United States of America

9 2023

Library of Congress Cataloging-in-Publication Data has been applied for.

ISBN 978-1-4405-9845-6
ISBN 978-1-4405-9846-3(ebook)

Contains material adapted from *The Everything® American Government Book* by Nick Ragone, copyright © 2004 by Simon & Schuster, Inc., ISBN 13: 978-1-59337-055-8; and *The Everything® U.S. Constitution Book* by Ellen M. Kozak, copyright © 2011 by Simon & Schuster, Inc., ISBN 13: 978-1-4405-1274-2.

CONTENTS

INTRODUCTION

Have you ever wondered just what the qualifications are to be president of the United States? Have you been curious about the Electoral College—what it is and why we have it? Are you curious about how Congress creates laws?

If so, *American Government 101* is for you. Here you'll learn, in clear, simple language, how American government works—from presidential elections to your local town council elections. You'll find entries that cover such topics as:

- What's really in the Constitution
- The role of the Senate and the House of Representatives
- The daily life of the president
- The powers of a state governor
- How federal, state, and city elections are conducted

It's important to know these things because the United States expects its citizens to participate in governing. After all, not only do Americans regularly select representatives in city, state, and federal government, but the American people also vote on an often-bewildering array of issues, ordinances, and initiatives. The better the American people are informed about how their government works, the better decisions they'll make about how it *should* work.

Understanding governmental institutions often seems challenging because of the sheer size of the government. When the House of Representatives met for the first time on March 4, 1789, it had just twenty-nine members; today it contains 435 (as well as six nonvoting members). As of 2014, the federal government employed approximately 4,185,000 people. In 1789, the entire population of the newly formed United States was only 3,929,000.

Apart from sheer numbers, the American government has become increasingly complicated. Although it may be hard to believe, the first Congress didn't have political parties; the national founders disapproved of them and hoped to avoid them. Today, it's impossible to imagine the U.S. governmental system without them. Reports of discussion in the House and Senate are dotted with references to "filibusters," "whips," "cloture," "Blue Dog Democrats," "Tea Party Republicans," and more.

While this sounds complicated, this book will help you make sense out of the government, whether it's in Washington, D.C., or in your local town hall. It will show you things like how a bill becomes a law, what's needed to pass and ratify a constitutional amendment, and much more. It will explain to you the complex rules of procedure followed by the Senate and the House, and how politicians use these to craft legislation.

Above all, this book will explain government to you as it *really* works. It will discuss the importance of money in politics and how it became such a major ingredient. This book will tell you about lobbyists: who they are and what they do. It will outline controversial Supreme Court decisions, from *Brown v.*

Board of Education to *Obergefell v. Hodges*, and explain why these decisions were so controversial.

The Founding Fathers of the United States didn't anticipate all the twists and turns the country's history would take. But Washington, Jefferson, Adams, Madison, and others were confident that the government they had created would be sufficient to cope with even the greatest crises and survive. So far, after more than two centuries, the government has done just that.

THE MAYFLOWER COMPACT AND COLONIAL GOVERNMENT

The Beginning of Self-Rule

The story of American government dates back to the earliest settlement of North America. Our grade-school textbooks taught us that the first settlers were religious separatists who came to America to escape the Church of England. Some did seek religious freedom; others sought a new beginning; and still others were simply attracted to adventure. A few were even fortune seekers.

EARLY ARRIVALS

The earliest English settlement took place at Roanoke Island, North Carolina. Established by English explorers in the mid- to late 1580s, the Roanoke Island colony is best remembered for its mysterious and sudden demise.

The British government set up a trading outpost at Jamestown, Virginia, in 1607. Although the colony managed to survive for two decades, it had to contend with harsh conditions and hostile Indians. Jamestown did leave an important legacy, however: The colonists adopted a representative assembly to govern their affairs.

The year 1620 saw the establishment of a colony in New England, when the Puritans crossed the Atlantic and landed in Plymouth, Massachusetts. The Crown did not charter these pilgrims; rather, they were fleeing England in search of freedom to practice their religion.

Before Plymouth

The New World wasn't the first haven the Puritans sought. Before setting out from England for America, the Puritans made their way to Holland. They lived there from 1606 to 1620 but found the Dutch language hard to understand and the relatively free ways of the Netherlands not to their liking. After much negotiation with various English and Dutch companies, they received a grant of land in the Virginia territory. However, they missed their destination and instead arrived first at Cape Cod and subsequently at Plymouth Bay.

Before touching land, forty-one men on board their ship, the *Mayflower*, signed the Mayflower Compact—a social contract that bound them to obey the authority of whatever government was established on land. Though the compact wasn't a constitution, it did have a profound impact on future generations of colonists, because it established the precedent that any governing authority in the New World requires the consent of the people. This powerful notion would spread throughout the colonies.

"Having undertaken, for the Glory of God, and advancements of the Christian faith and honor of our King and Country, a voyage to plant the first colony in the Northern parts of Virginia, do by these presents, solemnly and mutually, in the presence of God, and one another, covenant and combine ourselves together into a civil body politic; for our better ordering, and preservation and furtherance of the ends aforesaid; and by virtue hereof to enact, constitute, and frame, such just and equal laws, ordinances, acts, constitutions, and offices, from time to time, as shall be thought most meet and convenient for the general good of the colony; unto which we promise all due submission and obedience."

—From the Mayflower Compact

THE COLONIES FLOURISH

Settlements in Virginia and Massachusetts Bay were swiftly followed by more ships from England bearing colonists. By 1732, all of the original thirteen colonies were established. Though technically governed by London, the colonies enjoyed an enormous amount of autonomy. All thirteen had popularly elected legislatures that passed laws, levied taxes, and set policy, and each also had a formal governing document that resembled a constitution. For instance, Connecticut had the Fundamental Orders, Pennsylvania passed the Frame of Government, and Massachusetts adopted the Body of Liberties.

KINDS OF COLONIES

From the point of view of government, the American colonies fell into three categories. New Hampshire, New York, Virginia, North Carolina, and South Carolina were royal colonies, which had royal governors appointed by the king. The governor could call a local assembly, to which he acted as an adviser. Pennsylvania, New Jersey, and Maryland were proprietary colonies, in which the governor was appointed by the lord proprietor rather than the king. Massachusetts, Rhode Island, and Connecticut were charter colonies, in which legislative functions stemmed from letters patent (a type of written legal instrument) issued by the Crown. Massachusetts changed in 1684 from a charter colony to a royal colony.

Given its vast distance from the New World, and its abiding interest in commerce with the colonies, Britain found the system of home rule equally agreeable.

PRELUDE TO A REVOLUTION

Relations between the colonies and Britain remained smooth through the mid-1750s, until the French and Indian War. Although ultimately victorious, the tremendous cost of waging this seven-year war left England virtually bankrupt. Parliament decided to replenish Britain's treasury by taxing the colonies, something it hadn't done before.

Beginning in 1763, the British Parliament imposed a series of taxes and demands on the colonies, including the Sugar Act, the Townshend Acts, the Quartering Act, and the Stamp Act. The colonies rallied around the idea of "no taxation without representation" and began to boycott British goods, effectively forcing the British Parliament to repeal the taxes, except for a tax on tea. For the first time, the colonies had acted in unison to thwart Britain's will. This was an important first step toward gaining independence.

REBELLION AND REVOLUTION

The Shot Heard 'Round the World

During the 1760s and 1770s, tensions grew between the American colonies and His Majesty's government in London. Things came to a boiling point in 1773, when a group of patriots called the Sons of Liberty, protesting the tax on tea, boarded three British ships and dumped 342 chests of tea into Boston Harbor. In response to what was called the Boston Tea Party, King George III quarantined Boston Harbor and seized control of Boston's government.

THE STRUGGLE FOR INDEPENDENCE

Alarmed by the developments in Massachusetts, the colonies convened the First Continental Congress in Philadelphia on September 4, 1774. Independence and revolution were not on the agenda. The primary action was the adoption of a Declaration of Rights and Grievances, which reiterated the colonists' opposition to taxes and reasserted their right to home rule. The representatives of the states, or delegates, also agreed to boycott British goods and raise their own troops. Ultimately, their goal was to reclaim Colonial autonomy.

By the time the delegates gathered for the Second Continental Congress in the spring of 1775, fighting had already begun between the colonists and the British army. Skirmishes had taken place at Lexington and Concord in Massachusetts, and the port of Boston was under British occupation. The Congress appointed George Washington commander in chief of the ragtag militia that had formed outside of Boston, even though there was no formal declaration of war against England.

With the colonists evenly divided between British loyalists and revolutionaries, heated debate engulfed the thirteen colonies. Virginian Thomas Paine brilliantly articulated the revolutionary cause in his pamphlet *Common Sense*, which sold more than 120,000 copies in the early months of 1776.

"It is infinitely wiser and safer, to form a constitution of our own in a cool deliberate manner, while we have it in our power, than to trust such an interesting event to time and chance."

—Thomas Paine, *Common Sense*

The Signing of the Declaration of Independence

Americans celebrate the Fourth of July as Independence Day, the day the Declaration of Independence was signed in Philadelphia. Although the Declaration of Independence was formally adopted on July 4, the delegates to the Second Continental Congress didn't actually sign the document until August 2. The exception was John Hancock, who probably *did* sign it on July 4.

The Declaration of Independence

In the spring of 1776, the Second Congress set out to formally declare its independence from Britain. Thomas Jefferson was assigned the task of drafting the document, which he presented to the full Congress in late June. After debate and revision, the Congress adopted Jefferson's Declaration of Independence, and with that step embarked on one of the most momentous experiments in all humankind.

The Declaration of Independence accomplished three things:

1. It laid out a new governing principle—specifically, that all persons are created equal with certain unalienable rights, and that governments derive their power from the consent of the governed.
2. It set forth a specific list of grievances against King George III.
3. It formally declared the colonies' independence from Britain.

Winning the War

King George III and the British Parliament expressed little concern over the colonists' declaration, and with good reason: Few believed that a disorganized militia of peasants and farmers could prevail over the greatest army in the world.

"These are the times that try men's souls. The summer soldier and the sunshine patriot will, in this crisis, shrink from the service of their country; but he that stands by it now, deserves the love and thanks of man and woman."

—Thomas Paine, *Common Sense*

For much of the war, the colonists suffered one defeat after another, overwhelmed by the better-trained, better-equipped, better-funded, and better-fed British army. On more than one occasion, it took everything George Washington could muster to keep the Continental Army from disbanding. But the revolutionary spirit gained momentum as the war progressed. With victories at places like Cowpens, South Carolina; Monmouth, New Jersey; and Saratoga, New York, the tide turned for the Continental Army. On October 19, 1781, George Washington defeated British General Charles Cornwallis at Yorktown, Virginia, forcing England to sue for peace. After six long years, the war was finally over.

ARTICLES OF CONFEDERATION

The First Attempt at Unification

Declaring independence from Britain was one thing; creating a new government was quite another. With the backdrop of war, the colonists hammered out the Articles of Confederation in only sixteen months (from July 1776 to November of the following year). It took longer to ratify: South Carolina was the first to sign in February 1778; Maryland was the last in March of 1781. During its short existence, the Articles would account for few successes and many failures.

A FLAWED DOCUMENT

As a governing document, the Articles of Confederation was flawed from the start. With the memory of British oppression still fresh, the colonists were wary of creating a strong central government. Most preferred a loose confederation of states, with the national government subordinate to them. In effect, they were trying to reproduce a system of local rule that prevailed prior to the French and Indian War.

The Articles created a unicameral (single body) legislature with limited authority. Each state had one vote in this Congress, and there was no independent executive or judiciary branch. Instead, the Congress appointed temporary officers to do this work. Major pieces of legislation, such as raising revenues or amending the Articles, required a unanimous vote, which meant that any one state held veto power over the national government. When the Congress was out of session—which was frequent—a conference of delegates from each state acted in its stead.

The Articles of Confederation lacked the power to perform the most basic tasks, such as regulating interstate commerce, establishing a national currency, taxing the people directly, enforcing treaties, raising revenues, or compelling the states to contribute monies to the national government. As a consequence, the country was an economic wreck throughout its tenure. The Articles even struggled to maintain tranquility among the states. Toward the end of the war, things got so bad that the Congress was forced to sell off western lands just to pay for the militia. For all intents and purposes, the national government existed at the mercy of the states—a recipe for failure.

Shays's Rebellion

An uprising in western Massachusetts led by a bankrupt farmer named Daniel Shays finally convinced political leaders that the Articles of Confederation was ineffective. The rebellion marked the way in which economic difficulties were affecting ordinary people. The number of citizens in prison for debt had soared, and farms were being foreclosed on. Although it drew considerable popular support, Shays's Rebellion was put down in 1787, and it spurred political leaders to convene the Constitutional Convention the following year.

A FEW IMPORTANT ACHIEVEMENTS

While the Articles of Confederation was unquestionably a failure, it served to create a kind of "transition" government between the Revolutionary War and the birth of the republic as the country went through a "cooling off" period, with revolutionary zeal giving way to tempered reason. Leaders learned from its shortcomings and used the experience to create the Constitution. And it even had a few outright successes, such as the Land Ordinance of 1785 and the Northwest Ordinance of 1787, two major pieces of legislation that helped settle the West.

"The Articles of this Confederation shall be inviolably observed by every State, and the Union shall be perpetual; nor shall any alteration at any time hereafter be made in any of them; unless such alteration be agreed to in a Congress of the United States, and be afterwards confirmed by the legislatures of every State."

—The Articles of Confederation, Article XIII

But perhaps most important, the Articles of Confederation represents a milestone in the history of Western democracies. For the first time, citizens used reason and logic to create a new form of government. It was a bold and dramatic first step, and although it didn't succeed, it proved that a government of consent could be achieved through peaceful means. And it also gave our country its name: the United States of America.

WRITING THE CONSTITUTION

We, the People of the United States

In September of 1786, representatives from five states gathered in Annapolis, Maryland, to discuss amending the Articles of Confederation. Not long after convening, however, the group realized it would require delegates from all thirteen states to give the matter proper attention, so they decided to meet again in Philadelphia the following year.

Fifty-five delegates from twelve states (Rhode Island refused to attend) arrived in Philadelphia on May 25, 1787. The convention lasted the entire summer and was conducted in secret, as participants sought an honest exchange of ideas and compromise. As the first order of business, the delegates unanimously voted George Washington convention chair. It would be the only unanimous agreement.

On the Campaign Trail

George Washington is the only president of the United States to have been elected unanimously. All other elections have been hotly contested, with both sides hurling accusations and epithets at one another.

VIRGINIA AND NEW JERSEY PLANS

Shortly after the convention convened, Virginians James Madison and Edmund Randolph, two of the most well-respected attendees, submitted a constitutional proposal called the Virginia Plan, which was a radical departure from the Articles of Confederation. At the heart of the Virginia Plan was a bicameral (two-chamber) legislature with the lower house chosen by the people and the upper house chosen by the lower house. The plan also called for a national executive and judiciary, both of which were to be selected by the legislature. The Virginia Plan was a bold attempt at creating a strong central government.

While delegates from the large states supported the Virginia Plan, representatives from the smaller states complained that the larger states would dominate the national legislature (the number of legislative representatives would be determined by population). Other delegates feared that such a strong central government would snuff out states' rights and restrict individual liberty.

After weeks of heated debate, William Paterson of New Jersey hastily submitted an alternative document dubbed the New Jersey Plan. The New Jersey Plan was a modification of the Articles of Confederation. It called for a unicameral legislature with equal representation for each state regardless of population, a weak two-person executive branch, and a single judiciary body. Small-state delegates and weak-government proponents rallied around the New Jersey Plan, while big-state members stood firmly opposed.

THE GREAT COMPROMISE

Delegates were at a stalemate over the two proposals. In late July, Roger Sherman of Connecticut broke the impasse with a compromise known as the Connecticut Compromise. Sherman's compromise adopted the bicameral legislature approach of the Virginia Plan (with its population-based lower chamber) and the independent upper chamber (with equal representation) of the New Jersey Plan. Small-state delegates were satisfied with the equal representation of the upper chamber (Senate), while big-state representatives took solace in the population-based lower chamber (House).

With the framework of the Constitution in place, the delegates found common ground on the remaining issues. After rancorous debate, it was decided that the slave trade would remain legal until 1808, and that freed and escaped slaves would be returned to their owners.

Another issue related to slavery was how to count slaves for the census. Southerners wanted people of color counted equally in determining representation in Congress (because most slaves resided in the South), while Northerners argued that they shouldn't be counted at all. The delegates eventually agreed that slaves would be counted as three-fifths of a free person.

The delegates also came to agreement in selecting the chief executive. Many were opposed to having the president elected by the people, who were viewed as uneducated and uninformed. Others were adamant that the president should be chosen directly by the people. To solve the problem, the delegates came up with the Electoral College, which called for a separate body of "electors"—selected by each state's legislature—to ultimately vote for the president.

On September 17, 1787, thirty-nine of the remaining forty-two delegates signed the Constitution (some of the original fifty-five left early). The only remaining question was, would it be ratified?

THE PROCESS OF RATIFICATION

Ratification of the newly created Constitution was not a sure thing. There was a real concern that the document granted too much power to the federal government and would ultimately lead to aristocratic tyranny. Sensing the struggle that lay ahead, the framers wisely stated that the Constitution need only be approved by nine out of thirteen states. They also stipulated that the states would not vote on ratification through their state legislatures—which the founders feared would have great misgivings about the new central government—but rather through a special elective convention. Were it not for these two crucial provisions, the Constitution might not have been ratified at all.

Federalists and Antifederalists

Opinions regarding the Constitution were divided into two camps: the Federalists and antifederalists. The Federalists believed in a strong central government that shared powers with the states, and therefore they supported the Constitution. The antifederalists were suspicious of this new central government and preferred direct democracy and local rule. In the fall of 1787, each side began publishing essays in support of its position, and today these writings represent some of the most important (and most studied) discussions on American government and political theory.

"The operations of the federal government will be most extensive and important in times of war and danger; those of the State governments, in times of peace and security."

—James Madison, *The Federalist Papers*

The Federalists were led by James Madison, Alexander Hamilton, and John Jay, who together wrote *The Federalist Papers*. Two essays in particular—James Madison's Federalist No. 10 and Federalist No. 51—are cited as the most persuasive in support of the Constitution. The antifederalists were led by patriots such as Patrick Henry, John Hancock, George Mason, future president James Monroe, and Sam Adams.

RACE TO THE FINISH LINE

Beginning in the winter of 1787, state conventions began the process of ratification. The Constitution was officially ratified on June 21, 1788, when New Hampshire narrowly adopted it by a 57–46 vote. However, it wasn't until late July that it became clear the new union was destined to survive, when Virginia and New York, the two largest states at the time, approved the document. The following is the order of ratification:

1. Delaware, December 7, 1787
2. Pennsylvania, December 12, 1787
3. New Jersey, December 18, 1787
4. Georgia, January 2, 1788
5. Connecticut, January 9, 1788
6. Massachusetts, February 6, 1788
7. Maryland, April 28, 1788
8. South Carolina, May 23, 1788
9. New Hampshire, June 21, 1788
10. Virginia, June 25, 1788
11. New York, July 26, 1788
12. North Carolina, November 21, 1789
13. Rhode Island, May 29, 1790

And with that, the United States of America got a fresh start.

WHAT'S IN THE CONSTITUTION

Formula for Freedom

The structure of the Constitution is straightforward and simple. It establishes the three branches of government—legislative, executive, and judicial—and their powers and requirements. It also creates the system of "checks and balances" that defines American government.

"We the People of the United States, in Order to form a more perfect Union, establish Justice, insure domestic Tranquility, provide for the common defence, promote the general Welfare, and secure the Blessings of Liberty to ourselves and our Posterity, do ordain and establish this Constitution for the United States of America."

—The Constitution, Preamble

ARTICLE I: LEGISLATIVE BRANCH

Article I is the longest of the seven articles that compose the Constitution. It consists of ten sections, some of which are further subdivided by clauses.

Creating the House and Senate

Article I, Section 1 of the Constitution establishes the Congress as the first branch of government. Section 2 establishes the House of

Representatives. Clauses 1 and 2 lay out the qualifications for serving in the House of Representatives, and the process for House elections.

On the Campaign Trail

The framers left it up to the states to determine who may vote for members of Congress. Prior to the Civil War, most states restricted voting to white male property owners over the age of twenty-one. Over time, the property requirement was dropped, and African Americans, other minorities, and women were granted voting rights.

A state's representation in the House is based on its population size. The Constitution guarantees that each state will have at least one representative, and it originally called for one representative for every 30,000 citizens. That number has increased to 600,000 citizens over the years. Today, the number of representatives is capped at 435. Section 2 also states that when a vacancy occurs in the House, the state's governor must call a special election to fill it. Clause 5 gives the House—and only the House—the power to impeach (bring formal charges against) elected officials.

Section 3 establishes the United States Senate. Originally, the Constitution called for senators to be chosen by their respective state legislatures. The framers did this because they wanted the Senate to be a place where issues could be deliberated freely without the specter of electoral politics. They also gave senators six-year terms instead of two-year, which they thought would further remove them from the popular passions of the day.

Section 3 also establishes qualification for office, Senate leadership, the role of the vice president, impeachment trials, and the penalty for impeachment conviction. Under Clause 7 of Section 3, the only penalty for impeachment is removal from office.

Provisions for Running the Show

The next three sections establish the procedures for operating both the House and the Senate. Some of the more interesting provisions include the following:

- Congress must assemble at least once a year.
- Both chambers may refuse to seat a member (refuse to recognize the election or appointment of a representative or senator). Although this is rarely done, it has occurred on occasion. After scandal-ridden Representative Adam Clayton Powell Jr. was elected to his twelfth term in 1968, Congress refused to seat him.
- Both chambers must publish a journal of their proceedings after each session.
- Neither chamber can recess for more than three days without the consent of the other chamber.
- Congressional salaries are paid by the Department of Treasury, not by the respective states.
- Members of Congress cannot be arrested or sued for things said during speeches and debates made in the Capitol building.
- Members of Congress cannot simultaneously hold another federal government position.

The Powers of Congress

Most scholars consider Sections 7 through 10 of Article I as the most important in the Constitution, because it outlines the Congress's powers and limitations. Three of the Section 8 clauses are considered the most important:

1. *Commerce Clause.* Clause 3 gives the Congress the power to regulate interstate commerce and trade with foreign nations. Over the years, the commerce clause has expanded to give Congress the ability to regulate the national economy.
2. *Declaring War.* Clause 11 gives Congress—not the president—the power to declare war. Since the Korean War, Congress and the president have struggled to find a balance between the right of the Congress to declare war and the role of the president as commander in chief.
3. *The Elastic Clause.* Clause 18 of Section 8 gives Congress the power to make all "necessary and proper" laws that would help execute the enumerated powers of the Constitution.

Section 8 prohibits Congress from passing any law that inflicts punishment on an individual without a trial or provides punishment for acts that weren't illegal when the act was committed. It also prohibits Congress from taxing commerce between the states.

ARTICLE II: EXECUTIVE BRANCH

The second article of the Constitution establishes the executive branch and defines the powers of the presidency.

Section 1

Section 1 of Article II establishes the office of the presidency, and the method for selecting the president—the Electoral College. The Electoral College is composed of electors who equal the number of representatives and senators from a state.

In Section 1, the framers gave Congress the power to determine when presidential elections are held and when the Electoral College meets. Congress set the Tuesday after the first Monday in November of every fourth year as the presidential election day, and the Monday after the second Wednesday in December for the meeting of the Electoral College. Finally, Section 1 established that the president's salary cannot be diminished during his term in office and that he cannot receive other forms of payment while in office.

Section 2

This section covers the following duties and limitations:

1. *Commander in Chief.* Clause 1 states, "The President shall be Commander in Chief of the Army and Navy of the United States, and of the Militia of the several States."
2. *Treaties and appointments.* The power to make treaties and appointments has been one of the president's most acted-upon constitutional powers.
3. *Filling vacancies.* When Congress is not in session, the president has the power to make temporary appointments without Senate approval. Known as recess appointments, these temporary appointments expire at the end of the Congressional term.

The Last Two Sections of Article II

Section 3 requires the president to give Congress information regarding the State of the Union, and Section 4 prescribes impeachment for all civil officers who commit high crimes or misdemeanors.

ARTICLE III: JUDICIAL BRANCH

Article III establishes the judicial branch of government and the federal court system. Congress created the lower court system (Judiciary Act of 1789). The framers also provided that federal judges would serve lifelong terms and that their pay could not be diminished. Federal judges can only be removed by impeachment and conviction.

Much of Article III is dedicated to the types of cases that can appear before the Supreme Court and the conduct of trials. Clause 3 provides that any person accused of a federal crime has the right to a jury trial in the state where the crime was committed.

The other notable provision of Article III is the definition and punishment for treason. Treason is defined as "giving aid and comfort" to the enemy or levying war against the United States.

ARTICLE IV: RELATIONS AMONG THE STATES

Article IV of the Constitution establishes the relationship among the states. Political authority is shared by the federal government and state governments. The framers settled on this system because it satisfied those delegates who believed a strong central government was necessary to create a union as well as those who wanted to preserve state autonomy.

The framers enumerated several key doctrines in Article IV that helped construct the federal model of government:

- *Full Faith and Credit Clause.* This clause mandates that the states respect each others' laws, legal decisions, and records, such as driver's license, marriage proceedings, divorce records, and the like.
- *Privileges and Immunities Clause.* This clause establishes that the citizens of one state should enjoy the rights and privileges that are accorded in the state that they happen to be in.
- *Extradition Clause.* Accused persons who flee to another state must be returned to the state where the crime was committed.
- *Admission of States.* Section 3 provides that only Congress can admit a new state into the Union.
- *Republican Form of Government.* Section 4 establishes three important doctrines. First, states must elect their government officials. Second, the federal government is bound to protect the states from foreign invasion. And third, the state governments can call upon the federal government to quell domestic violence within their states.

ARTICLE V: AMENDMENTS

The Constitution can be amended in one of two ways. The first (and more common) approach requires a two-thirds vote of each chamber of Congress, followed by ratification by three-fourths of all the state legislatures. The second approach requires two-thirds of the state legislatures to call for a constitutional convention. This method has never been tried.

Every section of the Constitution is subject to amendment except one: States must have equal representation in the United States Senate.

ARTICLE VI: NATIONAL SUPREMACY

This article, referred to as the supremacy clause, declares all federal laws take precedence over concurrent state laws.

Article VI also requires every federal and state official to pledge—with an oath—to support and uphold the Constitution of the United States, and it bans religion as a qualification to hold any federal or state office.

AMENDING THE CONSTITUTION

Protecting Our Rights

The founders made the Constitution difficult to amend precisely because they wanted its core to remain the same from generation to generation. They had enough confidence in the system of government they had designed that they didn't want subsequent politicians monkeying too much with it.

On the other hand, they recognized almost immediately that the document needed some additions, so as to protect the rights of Americans. Thus the first U.S. Congress agreed on ten amendments (pared down from twelve). These became known as the Bill of Rights.

The Bill of Rights has come to symbolize the ideal that forms the basis of the American system of government. While some Americans would have difficulty in pointing to the Constitution as the source of our system of checks and balances, far fewer would have trouble identifying the Bill of Rights as the repository of our basic freedoms.

HOW THE BILL WAS BORN

Contrary to common belief, the Bill of Rights did not introduce the concept of inalienable freedoms from government power. In fact, the early settlers and colonists began defining liberties shortly after setting foot in the New World.

Maryland passed the Toleration Act of 1649, becoming the first colony to codify religious liberty. The others soon followed suit. A decade earlier, Massachusetts had adopted the Body of Liberties, a rudimentary bill of rights that (although it was silent on religious freedoms) guaranteed the right to peaceably assemble, the right to a jury trial in civil cases, the equal protection of laws, and compensation for private property taken for public purposes, among other things. William Penn took it one step further, creating a long list of enumerated rights in Pennsylvania's first Constitution, which was adopted in 1682.

State Constitutions

Following the Declaration of Independence, the states began adopting new state constitutions. The first of these efforts, the Virginia Constitution of 1776, actually begins with a sixteen-point Declaration of Rights that restrained all three branches of government—executive, legislative, and judicial. It was the first to proclaim that all men are created equal and that all power derives from the people.

Pennsylvania's Bill of Rights introduced the separation of church and state, the right to counsel in criminal cases, the right to bear arms, and the right to travel. Delaware's Bill of Rights was the first to prohibit the quartering of troops in homes during peacetime, while Maryland's outlawed bills of attainder (acts of legislature that declare a person or group of persons guilty of some crime and punishing them, often without a trial).

On the Campaign Trail

One issue debated with great heat in the election of 1800 was the Alien and Sedition Acts. These acts, passed by Congress and signed into law by President John Adams in 1798, restricted immigration and made it possible for the government to throw people in jail for their speeches or writings. Most of the acts were repealed after the election of Thomas Jefferson as the nation's third president.

Massachusetts' Bill of Rights made an important contribution in outlawing all unreasonable searches and seizures, but more important was the method by which it was created. Unlike the other states, which created their bills of rights through the normal legislative process, Massachusetts was the first to call a special constitutional convention. By doing this, it established the precedent that the Bill of Rights could only be altered by constitutional convention.

As the states began deliberating the adoption of the newly created Constitution, the delegates quickly realized their political blunder in not including a bill of rights. Antifederalists used the lack of a bill of rights to rally the public against the Constitution. In response, James Madison and his fellow Federalists promised that the new Congress would create a bill of rights as its first order of business.

True to his word, Madison took up the issue of a bill of rights in the summer of 1789. Borrowing from state bills of rights and other public writings, Madison proposed seventeen amendments to the Constitution, which the House quickly passed. The Senate pruned the list, and the Bill of Rights was submitted to the states for ratification. On December 15, 1791, Virginia became the eleventh state to ratify ten amendments, and with that the United States Constitution had a Bill of Rights.

OTHER AMENDMENTS TO THE CONSTITUTION

In addition to the Bill of Rights, the United States Constitution has been amended seventeen times. The first additional amendment was made in 1795 and the last in 1992. Only one amendment to the

Constitution has been repealed—the eighteenth, which prohibited the production, sale, or transportation of alcohol.

Like the Bill of Rights, over the years some amendments have loomed larger in importance than others:

- *Thirteenth Amendment.* Ratified in December of 1865, it freed all slaves and abolished slavery in the United States and its territories. Former slaves were given the same rights as other citizens.
- *Fourteenth Amendment.* Ratified in 1868, the Fourteenth Amendment is both the longest and most frequently cited amendment in constitutional law. Initially passed to protect the rights of former slaves, over time the Fourteenth Amendment has evolved to mean that all citizens are subject to due process and equal protection of the laws.
- *Fifteenth Amendment.* Ratified in 1870, it states that "the right of citizens of the United States to vote shall not be denied or abridged by the United States or by any State on account of race, color, or previous condition of servitude." It wasn't until a year after the landmark Civil Rights Act of 1964, however, that true voting rights were established for all Americans.
- *Sixteenth Amendment.* Ratified in 1913, it overturned an 1894 Supreme Court decision that held income taxes to be unconstitutional. Essentially, this amendment allows Congress to tax income without apportioning the revenues evenly among the states.
- *Nineteenth Amendment.* Ratified just prior to the 1920 presidential election, it gave women the right to vote in state and federal elections. The amendment was first proposed in 1878, and came before Congress eight times before finally winning passage. A few states—Wyoming, Idaho, Utah, and Colorado—allowed

women to vote prior to the Nineteenth Amendment, but the majority did not.

- *Twenty-Second Amendment.* Ratified in 1951, it prohibited presidents from serving more than two elected terms. It also stipulates that if a president succeeds to office after the halfway point of his predecessor's term, he can serve two more elected terms (for a total of ten years in office). This amendment was a direct response to Franklin Roosevelt's four terms in office, which many legislators considered excessive.
- *Twenty-Sixth Amendment.* Ratified in 1971, it established that citizens who are eighteen years of age or older cannot be denied the right to vote in federal or state elections by virtue of age. This amendment was largely a response to discontent stemming from the Vietnam War, during which thousands of teenagers died on the battlefield.

FREEDOM OF SPEECH AND PRESS

The Cornerstones of American Freedom

It's no coincidence that the First Amendment appears at the top of the list. The framers believed that free speech, free religious expression, and a free press were critical to democracy, and an essential component of liberty. The First Amendment provides some of our most cherished freedoms.

At the time of the framing of the Constitution, freedom of the press referred to newspapers and pamphlets. Today, it applies to multiple media—television, radio, Internet, magazines, e-mail, billboards, and so on.

Over the years, the Supreme Court has interpreted freedom of the press broadly, putting few restrictions on the media. In 1971, the Supreme Court denied President Nixon an injunction against the *New York Times* from publishing a classified report (known as the Pentagon Papers, which it had obtained from a disgruntled former Defense Department employee) that detailed the role of the United States in the Vietnam War. The court ruled that such an injunction would violate the First Amendment.

FREEDOM OF SPEECH

Is there an absolute right to free speech, or may the government curtail certain types of speech and expression? In a landmark Supreme Court case in 1919, legendary Justice Oliver Wendell Holmes Jr.

created the "clear and present danger test" for free speech. The doctrine allows the government to curtail or limit speech if it can demonstrate that the speech represents a clear and present danger to public safety.

The courts have been unwilling to extend constitutional protection to speech that is considered slanderous or obscene. Defining and regulating obscene speech has been particularly difficult for the courts, as Supreme Court Justice Potter Stewart all but admitted when he wrote in a 1964 decision that, although he couldn't define obscenity, "I know it when I see it."

Restraints and Defamation

With every right comes a certain amount of responsibility. There are three basic restraints on the freedom to express yourself. The first of these is social responsibility. This was perhaps best summed up by Justice Oliver Wendell Holmes Jr., in 1919. In the case of *Schenck v. United States*, "The most stringent protection of free speech would not protect a man falsely shouting fire in a theater and causing a panic."

There is also the problem of defamation. Defamation is a civil wrong, committed against another person or group, rather than against society as a whole. If you publish something false about another person, and the defamation causes that person harm or economic loss, you can be made to compensate the person you have defamed. This is a balancing act, such as in this analogy: Your right to swing your arm ends where your fist collides with another person's nose.

On the Campaign Trail

In 2009, after prolonged argument, the Supreme Court issued a ruling in the case of *Citizens United v. Federal Election Commission*. The ruling, which was 5–4, effectively struck down much legislation having to do with campaign finance reform. The majority argued, against vigorous dissent led by Justice David Souter, that limiting the amount of money that could be spent to support candidates was, in effect, a limitation on freedom of speech.

Copyright

A third restriction on freedom of speech lies in one of the other areas of Congressional power: copyright. The first U.S. copyright law was passed by the First Federal Congress, in 1789. The United States is signatory to the Berne Convention for the Protection of Literary and Artistic Works, a multinational treaty that, because it was ratified by the Senate in 1989, is now part of U.S. law. As a consequence of U.S. copyright law and U.S. membership in the Berne Convention, you cannot reproduce the copyrighted work (whether photograph, illustration, music, audiovisual work, text, or a combination of those) owned by another person without that person's permission.

FREEDOM TO BEAR ARMS

Security versus Gun Violence

The Second Amendment ranks among the most contentious provisions in the Constitution. It simply states: "A well regulated Militia, being necessary to the security of a free State, the right of the people to keep and bear Arms, shall not be infringed."

The ambiguity of the amendment's wording has preoccupied constitutional scholars—and others—for years. Does it mean that everyone in the United States is entitled to own a gun? Does it mean that the Constitution favors the establishment and maintenance of a band of citizen soldiers and that owning guns is part of their requisite equipment? Are, perhaps, the two parts not related at all? Are they just two unrelated statements—that militias are a good thing, and so is owning a weapon (if you want to do so)?

The meaning of the "right to keep and bear arms" in 1789 meant a flintlock rifle, not an Uzi. The word in the Constitution is "arms." Could this mean a Taser, or a blowgun? Or perhaps a lightsaber?

In 2008, in *District of Columbia v. Heller*, the Supreme Court struck down an ordinance that restricted gun ownership by individuals. The court held that under the Second Amendment, individuals, even those not affiliated with a militia, can own guns for hunting and self-defense in a federal enclave.

However, the court indicated that it did not mean that the government could not impose some restrictions on gun ownership; for example, the right of convicted felons and the mentally ill to possess guns. It also did not ban the prohibition of guns in schools and other public buildings, nor did it mean to ban the kinds of guns not normally used for self-defense (such as automatic or semiautomatic weapons). Additionally, because this case struck down a District of Columbia (federal) rule, the court did not decide whether the Second Amendment is, by virtue of the incorporation or other doctrine, applicable to state law concerning gun control as well.

While the Supreme Court has generally come down in favor of an interpretation of the amendment that widens access to firearms by the population, many state and city ordinances have sprung up to regulate access to weapons. Among these are background checks, which are generally regulated state by state. The purpose of these checks is to avoid guns falling into the hands of violent criminals or people with a history of mental illness.

Newtown Shooting

One powerful catalyst for gun control reform occurred on December 14, 2012, when Adam Lanza, a mentally ill young man, shot and killed twenty students and six adults at Sandy Hook Elementary School in Newtown, Connecticut. The tragedy spurred intense national debate about expanding universal background checks as well as banning certain weapons such as those with magazines containing more than ten rounds of ammunition.

Opponents of the checks have argued that they are ineffective and would not have prevented most mass shootings in the United States during the past several decades. Instead, the National Rifle Association (NRA) and others have argued that the solution to the gun issue in the United States is more guns. If more citizens were armed and trained in the use of weapons, they claim, fewer criminals would attack.

SEPARATION OF CHURCH AND STATE

The Establishment Clause

The First Amendment begins with the following: "Congress shall make no law respecting an establishment of religion, or prohibiting the free exercise thereof." The language of the amendment does two things: It prohibits the government from creating an "official" religion (establishment clause), and prevents the government from prohibiting the practice of any religion (free exercise clause). Over the years, the Supreme Court has interpreted the establishment clause to mean that the federal and state governments cannot set up a church, give preference to one religion over another, participate in the affairs of religious organizations, or punish individuals because of their religious beliefs. The issue of prayer in public schools is an example of the difficult application of the First Amendment to everyday scenarios, because some people argue it violates the establishment clause.

The Ten Commandments in the Courtroom

In the summer of 2003, Alabama Supreme Court Chief Justice Roy Moore created a national stir when he refused a federal court order to remove a 5,300-pound stone engraving of the Ten Commandments from a state judicial building. (Later, Moore was removed from the bench by a Court of the Judiciary. However, he won re-election to the post of chief justice in 2012.) It wasn't Moore's first brush with controversy; eight years earlier, the American Civil Liberties Union (ACLU) had sued him for posting the Ten Commandments in his courtroom.

On the other hand, the free exercise clause prevents the government from restricting religious practices. Broadly speaking, the government cannot ban religious practices or interfere with citizens' religious beliefs. The courts have ruled that children cannot refuse certain types of medical vaccinations, even if it goes against their religious beliefs, arguing that it would jeopardize public safety. In 1993, Congress passed the Religious Freedom Restoration Act, which requires federal, state, and local governments to accommodate religious conduct in the least restrictive manner possible.

SEPARATION OF CHURCH AND STATE

Roger Williams, founder of the colony of Rhode Island, first used the phrase "a wall of separation" between church and state in a book published in 1644. Williams was particularly concerned with this principle, since he and others had founded Rhode Island after fleeing the theocracy established by the pilgrims in Massachusetts.

In 1802, Jefferson applied the term specifically to the provisions of the First Amendment in a letter to a group of Baptists who were concerned with privileges they thought were being granted to the Congregational church in Connecticut.

"Believing with you that religion is a matter which lies solely between man and his god, that he owes account to none other for his faith or his worship, that the legitimate powers of government reach actions only, and not opinions, I contemplate with sovereign reverence that act of the whole American people which declared that their 'legislature' should 'make no law respecting an establishment of religion, or prohibiting the free exercise thereof,' thus building a wall of separation between church and State. Adhering to this expression of the supreme will of the nation in behalf of the rights of conscience, I shall see with sincere satisfaction the progress of those sentiments which tend to restore to man all his natural rights, convinced he has no natural right in opposition to his social duties."

—Thomas Jefferson, Letter to Danbury Baptists

One of the reasons Jefferson, Madison, and others were concerned about this issue was the tremendous religious diversity represented by pre-revolutionary America. Not only were the major branches of Christianity well represented (as well as Judaism and Islam), but there were a wide variety of smaller dissenting sects that had sprung up, especially in the backwoods areas of the colonies. The Founding Fathers were, themselves, of a wide variety of religious beliefs. Some, such as Washington, were devout Christians; others such as Jefferson and Franklin were deists. Thomas Paine, author of *Common Sense*, was an agnostic.

SCHOOL PRAYER

During the eighteenth and nineteenth centuries, school days opened with a teacher-led prayer. This continued into the twentieth century, although dissenting voices were raised.

In 1955, after the New York Board of Regents developed a short, nondenominational prayer to be recited in New York's public schools, a group of parents of several different faiths challenged the board in court. The Supreme Court took up this and one other similar case in 1963 and issued a ruling prohibiting state sponsorship of prayer in school. Since then, there have been numerous battles of this and other parallel issues. All of them turn on the question, "Is the *state* sponsoring a religious activity?" Individual prayer or religious observance is still permitted in schools or on other public property as long as it does not have state endorsement.

THE HOUSE OF REPRESENTATIVES

The Lower House

The American Congress is made up of two houses—the House of Representatives and the Senate. In this system, the House is the governing body that is closest to the people. Whether it's healthcare insurance or increasing the minimum wage, popular issues do not reach critical mass until taken up in the House.

THE PEOPLE'S HOUSE

The House of Representatives is often referred to as "The People's House," because its members represent the smallest unit of the population. The typical House district encompasses approximately 600,000 people.

It is often the case that constituents in need turn to their House representative for assistance, whether in finding a lost social security check, helping a son or daughter get into a military academy, or navigating the federal bureaucracy. Not surprisingly, most members specialize in constituency casework. Over the course of their careers, many members will come to know thousands of their constituents by name—a surefire way to guarantee a long tenure in the House!

This is by design. The two-year terms, smaller districts, and direct election by the people were intended to make the House a populist institution. In fact, until the passage of the Seventeenth Amendment, ratified in 1917, which called for direct election of U.S. senators, the House of Representatives was the only branch of the federal government elected directly by the people.

On the Campaign Trail

The first woman elected to Congress was Jeannette Rankin, a Republican who captured Wyoming's lone House seat in 1916. An avowed pacifist, Rankin cast the only vote in Congress against the declaration of war on Japan. Rankin was easily defeated for re-election the following year.

TAKE ME TO YOUR LEADER

Congressional leadership is organized by party. Congressional leaders serve an important function within the institution (as parliamentarians) as well as "outside" the House in their efforts to recruit candidates, advocate policy positions in the media, raise money, and provide long-term political and policy strategy.

Speaker of the House

The Speaker of the House is the most powerful and visible member of the House of Representatives. It is the only House leadership position specifically accounted for in the Constitution. The Speaker stands third in line in presidential succession.

The Speaker is nominated by a majority of his party's caucus or membership at the beginning of each two-year session of Congress, and is formally elected by a straight-party vote of the entire House of Representatives. Rarely do members of the minority party cast a vote for the opposing party's Speaker designee.

The Speaker has the institutional powers to do the following:

- Determine committee assignments
- Preside over the House
- Decide on points of order and interpret the rules
- Refer legislation to the appropriate committees
- Set the agenda and schedule legislative action
- Coordinate policy agenda with Senate leadership

Speakers' strengths or weaknesses of personality often determines how effective they are. Republican Newt Gingrich was a formidable adversary to President Clinton, particularly on issues such as welfare reform, tax cuts, and balancing the budget. Republican John Boehner, during President Obama's presidency, on the other hand, resigned under pressure from members of his own party.

Majority and Minority Leaders

The majority leader is the principle deputy to the Speaker of the House, and the floor leader of the majority party. He is elected by a secret ballot of his party's caucus at the beginning of each two-year session of Congress. His primary function is to foster unity and cohesion among the majority members, and assist the Speaker in setting the agenda, scheduling debate, and monitoring the legislative process.

The minority leader is the leader of the opposition party in the House. His function is similar to that of majority leader—to maintain unity within his ranks. The minority leader will sometimes use procedural maneuvers and delaying tactics to "gum up" the legislative process in an effort to win concessions, make a point, seek compromise, or simply gain the attention of his counterparts.

Whips

Both the majority and minority leadership use "whips"—deputies who are responsible for maintaining party loyalty and "counting heads" on key votes. Whips are also elected by secret ballot, and are notorious for exerting pressure on their members to vote the party position.

HOUSE BY COMMITTEE

Although not specified in the Constitution, committees are where the substantive and legislative work of Congress takes place. Given the enormous complexity and diversity of issues that members confront each session, committees have evolved into specialized divisions of labor where members can concentrate on particular areas of expertise. As a general rule, each House member serves on two standing committees, although members of the three powerful Appropriations, Rules, and Ways and Means Committees serve only on those committees. Most House committees are divided into five subcommittees that focus on more specific areas.

Types of Committees

There are four primary types of committees in the House of Representatives.

1. *Standing Committees.* These are the permanent bodies of Congress where virtually all of the legislative action takes place. Standing committees are by far the most important structures in Congress. The following are the twenty standing committees of the 114th Congress:

   - Agriculture
   - Appropriations
   - Armed Services
   - Budget
   - Education and the Workforce
   - Energy and Commerce
   - Ethics
   - Financial Services
   - Foreign Affairs
   - Homeland Security
   - House Administration
   - Judiciary
   - Natural Resources
   - Oversight and Government Reform
   - Rules
   - Science, Space, and Technology
   - Small Business
   - Transportation and Infrastructure
   - Veterans' Affairs
   - Ways and Means

2. *Select or Special Committees.* These are temporary panels created from time to time to study or investigate a particular

problem or issue. They have a narrow focus and are usually disbanded at the end of the Congressional session in which they were created.

3. *Joint Committees.* These are composed of members from both the House of Representatives and Senate. Typically, they deal with administrative matters pertaining to Congress. Joint committees can be either permanent or temporary.

4. *Conference Committees.* These committees are also composed of House and Senate members, but they have the express purpose of standardizing the exact language of concurrent pieces of legislation that the two chambers have passed.

Joining a Committee

For members of Congress, committee assignments rank among the most important aspects of their job. The Speaker of the House and the minority leader determine assignments for their respective party members in conjunction with their steering committee, which is convened for that specific purpose.

The most important factor in committee assignments is seniority—the longer a member has served in Congress, the greater his or her chances of receiving a plum assignment. Some members receive committee assignments based on knowledge or expertise, while others are assigned based on the needs of his or her district (representatives from Midwestern states often serve on the Agriculture Committee, for instance). It's not unusual for members to receive a desired committee post as a reward for party loyalty or fundraising prowess, or for ideological reasons.

Committee Leaders

The most powerful member of any committee is the chairperson. The chair hires majority staff, appoints subcommittee members and leaders, and allocates the committee and subcommittee budgets. At one time, chairpersons dominated their committees like feudal lords, ruling with an iron fist. Recent reforms, however, have curbed their powers.

After taking power in 1994, the Republicans adopted term limits for their committee chairpersons, restricting their members to only three terms as a chairperson on a given committee. This limitation does not prohibit term-limited Republicans from serving as chairperson on another committee and does not apply to House Democrats.

RULES RULE

The large size and populist composition of the House of Representatives require that its activity be governed by a strict set of formal rules. Were it not for these rules, almost nothing would get accomplished in the unwieldy lower chamber.

The House rules that matter most are those that deal with legislative debate. At the request of the reporting committee's chairperson, the Rules Committee typically grants one of three rules that govern floor debate and the amendments process for a given piece of legislation:

1. An open rule allows for any amendments to be offered, as long as they are relevant to the subject of the bill.

2. A closed rule prohibits any amendments from being offered.
3. A modified rule allows amendments to be offered to some parts of the bill, but not others.

With the rise of partisanship over the past few years, the Rules Committee has begun to write more complex or "creative" rules in an effort to exert greater control over floor action. With names like the King-of-the-Hill Rule, the Multiple-Step Rule, the Self-Executing Rule, and the Anticipatory Rule, these rules are mostly used to keep unfriendly amendments from sinking a bill. More often than not, the type of rule a bill receives will determine the likelihood of its passage.

CLIQUES AND CAUCUSES

The first Congressional caucus was formed in 1959, and since that time the number has proliferated to more than 100 in the House of Representatives alone. Virtually every region, interest group, ethnicity, and cause has its own caucus, such as the Congressional Wine Caucus, Congressional Down Syndrome Caucus, Congressional Mining Caucus, the Friends of Norway Caucus, the Rural Health Caucus, Congressional Arts Caucus, and the Congressional Urban Caucus, to name but a few.

The two most recognized and influential caucuses in Congress are the Congressional Black Caucus and the Blue Dog Democrats. Both groups wield considerable power over the House Democrats. The Blue Dog Democrats are a group of fiscally conservative Democrats who frequently vote with the Republicans on economic matters.

In 2002, the Congressional Black Caucus played a pivotal role in ousting Senate Majority Leader Trent Lott from his leadership post after the Mississippi Republican made racially insensitive remarks.

SO YOU WANT TO BE A MEMBER?

Hundreds of candidates run for Congress every two years. Some seek the position as a steppingstone to higher office; others do it in order to effect change in a specific policy area; others are compelled by a sense of civic duty.

Eligibility Requirements

The Constitution lays out three requirements for gaining entry to the U.S. House of Representatives:

1. You must be twenty-five years old at the time of inauguration.
2. You must be a resident of the state in which your district resides.
3. You must have been a United States citizen for seven years prior to inauguration.

During the mid-1990s, several states tried to impose term limitations on their Congressional delegation, but the Supreme Court ruled that state-mandated term limits were unconstitutional. The high court held that Congressional term limits could be implemented only by amending the Constitution.

THE SENATE

America's Most Elite Club

The U.S. Senate is a unique institution in American government. The framers wanted one chamber of the legislature to remain insulated from the popular passions of the day, so that its members could deliberate and debate the great issues without fear of reprisals from voters.

COOLING OFF THE HOUSE

Until 1913, senators were selected by their state legislatures and not by the people. This distance from the people allowed the Senate to establish procedures that would safeguard minority rights in a way that the House could not. In fact, a handful of senators—and in some cases just one—have the ability to bring the body to a standstill through delaying tactics and unlimited debate.

Since the ascension of the presidency as the first branch of government, which began with Theodore Roosevelt, the Senate has lost some of its preeminence. It is less elitist and more populist today, but retains some important vestiges of its noble origins.

WHO RUNS THIS PLACE?

The nature and style of leadership in the Senate is dramatically different than that of the lower chamber. The House requires a rigid hierarchy of leaders and deputy leaders who enforce strict discipline to get anything accomplished. The Senate takes the opposite approach. With only 100 members, leadership can be more collegial and informal.

Floor Leaders

Although the Constitution provides that the vice president shall serve as the Senate president, it's mostly a symbolic title. The only time the vice president presides over the Senate is to cast the occasional tie-breaking vote.

When the vice president is absent, which is usually the case, the Senate president pro tempore (also known as the pro tem) presides over the chamber. The pro tem position is typically held by the member of the majority party with the longest continuous service in the Senate. Like the role of the vice president, it is mostly a ceremonial position. However, it does carry one important function: The pro tempore is fourth in line to the presidency behind the vice president and Speaker of the House.

Real leadership in the Senate is provided by the majority and minority leaders elected by their respective party's caucus, along with whips, who serve as their deputies. Given the shortage of formal rules, and the ability of the minority to obstruct floor action, the two leaders are forced to work more closely together than their House counterparts.

The most important power the leaders enjoy is the right of first recognition, meaning they are allowed to speak first during floor debate. It gives leaders the ability to outflank their adversaries by shaping the debate, offering amendments, and making other motions to reconsider.

On the Campaign Trail

In 1964 Robert F. Kennedy, who had left the office of attorney general shortly after the assassination of his brother, announced he would seek a Senate seat from New York State. There was much complaining, mixed with amusement, since it was well known that the Kennedys were based in Massachusetts. However, New York voters ignored this point and elected Kennedy.

When the majority leader is a member of the president's party, he acts as the legislative point man for the White House and is expected to mobilize support for the president's agenda. The opposition leader is expected to thwart the president's agenda, more so than the House opposition leader, who has few tools at his disposal to derail the majority.

Committee Chairmen

Senate committee chairmen are elected by a majority of their caucuses, although their election is in keeping with the seniority system. Typically, the majority member with the longest tenure on a committee is automatically elevated to chairman, subject to caucus approval.

JOINING THE CLUB

The Seventeenth Amendment to the Constitution, which changed the process of selecting senators, did not, however, alter the formal qualifications established in the Constitution for becoming a member. Senators still must be thirty years of age or older and a United States citizen for nine years prior to election, and they must be residents of the state they represent.

Money, Money, Money

Although anyone who meets the age, citizenship, and residency requirements can run for the United States Senate, the most important requirement is money—and lots of it. Based on 2013 data from the Federal Election Commission, the average senatorial candidate spends $10.5 million during each campaign in hopes of achieving victory (as opposed to $1.7 million to run for a seat in the House).

Over the past decade, there has been a surge in the number of wealthy individuals who have sought Senate seats, and approximately one-third of the chamber is now composed of millionaires. Outside of the super-wealthy who can finance their own campaigns, most members spend anywhere from a quarter to a third of their time raising money for re-election.

Even though the Seventeenth Amendment has opened up the electoral process, the skyrocketing cost of Senate campaigns has dramatically limited the composition of the Senate. It has become increasingly difficult for ordinary citizens to mount credible campaigns.

PRESIDENTIAL DREAMING

There's an often-told joke in Washington about how every time a senator looks in the mirror, he sees a president staring back. Perhaps that's a bit of an exaggeration, but it contains a kernel of truth. At one time or another, most senators have visions of occupying the White House.

Even so, it's rarely a direct route. Though many have tried, only three sitting senators have been elected president: Warren G. Harding, John F. Kennedy, and Barack Obama. In total, sixteen presidents have been members of the Senate at some point in their careers, with six (the ones listed in bold) having served as vice president:

1. James Monroe
2. John Quincy Adams
3. Andrew Jackson
4. **Martin Van Buren**
5. William Henry Harrison
6. **John Tyler**
7. Franklin Pierce
8. James Buchanan
9. **Andrew Johnson**
10. Benjamin Harrison
11. Warren G. Harding
12. **Harry S. Truman**
13. John F. Kennedy
14. **Lyndon B. Johnson**
15. **Richard M. Nixon**
16. Barack Obama

While ten senators became presidents in the nineteenth century, only five accomplished the feat in the twentieth century (and so far, one in the twenty-first century). In recent years, the governor's mansion has replaced the Senate seat as the most reliable path to the White House. Voters seem to be placing less emphasis on legislative experience and more emphasis on executive experience, which is something the Senate does not provide.

ADVISE AND CONSENT AND FILIBUSTER

The Powers of the Senate

The Senate enjoys two constitutional prerogatives that set it apart from the House of Representatives. It alone has the authority to advise and consent on the president's appointments and treaties, as well as to conduct impeachment trials for federal officials. Both powers are exercised sparingly, but with dramatic impact.

THE POWER TO ADVISE AND CONSENT

The "advise and consent" provision in the Constitution is the Senate's most powerful check on the president. Over the years, it has been a steady source of friction between the upper chamber and the White House, and at times has put a severe strain on the relationship.

Treaties in the Senate

Since 1789, the Senate has rejected twenty-one treaties, the most notable being the Treaty of Versailles, which it voted against in 1919 and 1920. As a consequence, the United States did not join the League of Nations, which was the precursor to the United Nations. This was a huge defeat and embarrassment for President Woodrow Wilson, who had helped create the League following World War I.

During each session of Congress, the Senate approves thousands of presidential appointments—ambassadors, federal judges, Supreme Court justices, cabinet members, and other executive branch officials. Over the course of a single term, a president can make up to 35,000 military and civilian appointments that require Senate confirmation.

In recent years, the confirmation process for presidential nominations has become more contentious. For a long time, the Senate focused solely on the qualifications and competency of presidential appointments when considering approval, with the result being that very few nominees were rejected. But with the rise in partisan tension and the growing trend toward divided government, the confirmation process has become more politicized. Such was the situation for Judge Robert Bork, who, in 1987, was nominated to the Supreme Court and rejected by the Senate because his viewpoints were considered by some to be out of the mainstream. A couple of years later, Justice Clarence Thomas narrowly avoided a similar fate in one of the most vitriolic and divisive confirmation hearings in history. In many ways, the confirmation power has become the most potent political weapon the Senate wields against the president.

SUBJECT TO DEBATE

The Senate's tradition of unlimited debate dates back to the first Congress, when a handful of senators used stalling tactics to defeat a proposal to move the capital from New York City to Philadelphia. Since then, the practice of unlimited debate has been one of the most cherished rights in the Senate, and is the most distinguishing characteristic that sets it apart from the House of Representatives.

What's a Filibuster?

When unlimited debate is used to defeat a bill, it is called a *filibuster*. Filibustering typically involves endless speech on the Senate floor by a member or members, and may also include a series of delaying tactics such as calling for consecutive roll calls, raising points of order, and offering irrelevant amendments.

Filibustering is a highly effective mechanism for senators to defeat legislation or win concessions on nonrelated issues, especially if employed late in the session when there is insufficient time to break it. If timed correctly, the mere threat of a filibuster can be an effective negotiating tool. In some cases, senators will block legislation simply by asking their party leaders not to schedule the matter. This is called a *hold*, and using the hold is a custom honored by Senate leaders.

In 1917, at the urging of President Woodrow Wilson, the Senate amended its rules to provide a means for cutting off debate. Rule 22 (or *cloture*, as it is known) is invoked when three-fifths of the members present vote in favor of ending debate. Once cloture is adopted, senators have thirty hours of remaining debate before a final vote is taken.

Unanimous Consent Agreements

One way the Senate avoids the cycle of endless filibusters and cloture is through unanimous consent agreements. These are agreements that the majority and minority leaders make regarding the length of debate, the number and types of amendments that can be offered, and the time of final vote for a particular piece of legislation. As its name suggests, a unanimous consent agreement requires the full consent of every senator present—one "nay" vote kills the agreement. Most Senate business is conducted according to unanimous consent agreements.

CONGRESSIONAL DUTIES AND RESPONSIBILITIES

What Do These People *Do*?

Congress is in session throughout the year, with several scheduled recesses. Under normal circumstances, the House of Representatives is in session from Tuesday through Thursday, with members back in their districts the remainder of the time. The Senate, on the other hand, is typically in session the entire week; thus most senators travel home less frequently than do their House counterparts (unless it's an election year).

WHAT MEMBERS DO

While Congress is in session, a typical day for a member may include up to a dozen activities:

- Attending committee and subcommittee meetings and hearings
- Meeting with staff and other members to discuss pending legislation
- Participating in floor debate and voting on legislation
- Meeting with constituents and performing casework
- Caucusing with party members to devise legislative strategies
- Meeting with other government officials, interest groups, and lobbyists to discuss pending legislation

- Managing the staff and office operations
- Making media appearances to advance a piece of legislation or advocate a policy position

All of those are just the normal activities of the business day. After-hours duties may include attending fundraisers and other political events, preparing for the next day's activities, making phone calls to contributors and supporters back home, and traveling to other districts in support of party colleagues.

Most members spend their weekends in their district participating in town hall meetings, meeting with constituents, holding office hours, making public appearances, and attending political events. Between work and travel, there is little time for anything else.

THE CONGRESSPERSON'S ROLES

Congresspersons serve in many capacities. All of their responsibilities may be seen as fitting into four primary roles: legislator, constituent servant, representative, and educator.

Legislator

This is the most important role for any member of Congress. Representatives and senators cast thousands of votes each session. Most votes are on procedural matters, some are on legislative issues, and a few are on appointments and confirmations. Tax cuts, healthcare reform, and entitlement spending are just a few of the issues that members vote on every year, with financial implications running in the trillions of dollars.

Constituent Servant

Members are expected to intervene on behalf of their constituents to help solve problems, promote local businesses and commerce, bring money and projects back to the district, and explain the meaning of legislation to affected interest groups.

Representative

This role pertains to the congresspersons' duty to understand and represent the views of their constituents in Washington—one of the cornerstones of a republican government. Members usually adopt one of two approaches when discharging their representative duty. Some (most often senators) take a broader or "trustee" view of representation, meaning that they put the interests of the country before the narrow needs of their district or state. Other members (most often representatives) believe that their votes should mirror the views of their constituents, even if it's in conflict with their own beliefs. Most members will vary their approach depending on the issue.

Educator

Finally, members have a duty to educate the public about the issues that are before the Congress. They typically keep their constituents informed through newsletters, office hours in the district, town hall meetings, direct mail, and media appearances.

MAKING DECISIONS

A majority of the votes that take place in Congress occur along straight party lines, meaning that an overwhelming number of Republicans vote one way, and a majority of Democrats the other way. This should come as no surprise, considering that the primary function of Congressional leaders and whips is to enforce party discipline during votes. As a result, party affiliation is the best indicator of a member's vote.

On the Campaign Trail

Congressional votes can and do come back to haunt candidates for the presidency. John Kerry and Hillary Clinton both voted for the war in Iraq before coming out against it. Kerry's 2004 campaign for president struggled—unsuccessfully—to overcome the image of him as a flip-flopper.

Constituency

In some cases, members will take into account the views of their constituents when considering legislation. This is especially true if it's a high-profile or polarizing issue such as gun control, abortion, tax cuts, or sending troops abroad. It's not unusual for members to vote against their own beliefs if it's in conflict with their constituents' viewpoint.

Presidential Pressure

Although members of Congress pride themselves on their independence from the executive branch, presidential persuasion weighs heavily on key Congressional votes. Historically, when the president has an announced position on an issue, he prevails on about 75 percent of the Congressional votes.

As a general rule, the more popular the president, the more "persuadable" the Congress. President Lyndon Johnson was particularly adept at using presidential pressure (some would call it arm-twisting) to gain support from Congressional Democrats for his Great Society programs, civil rights initiative, and the war in Vietnam.

Vote Trading

Sometimes lawmakers will strike deals with other members to cast a vote a certain way in return for the same consideration on a future vote. Most vote trading takes place on low-profile and procedural matters—rarely on highly public issues. Vote trading is particularly common when a member is trying to take a spending project back to his or her district.

Ideology

In some cases, members will vote according to deeply held ideological or philosophical beliefs about the role of government. Sometimes ideological voting is consistent with straight-party voting. At other times, depending on the issue, ideological voting splits across party lines. This often is the case with First Amendment, abortion, and gun control legislation.

WORKING WITH OTHERS

The Congress interacts with the other branches and institutions of government on a regular basis. Three relationships in particular—the president, the courts, and the bureaucracy—help define the various powers and roles of Congress.

The President

Since the inception of the republic, the relationship between the Congress and the president has been a complex one. There has always been a natural tension between the two as each has struggled to gain dominance over the other.

The Founding Fathers believed that the best way to avoid oppressive and unjust rule was by making it difficult for government to act at all. They also believed that the real threat of tyranny lies with the president, not the Congress. Thus, they provided for a strong Congress with many enumerated powers and a relatively weak president with few specific powers.

Over the years, the balance of power has shifted between the two, with both branches enjoying preeminence at one time or another. The Congress held the upper hand for most of the nineteenth century as it overshadowed a succession of caretaker presidents, but since the presidency of Theodore Roosevelt, the White House has been the first branch of government. Its ascension was further spurred by four events: the Great Depression, World War II, the cold war, and the war on terrorism.

All through this, the relationship between the Congress and the president has alternated between cooperation and confrontation. Presidents with clear electoral mandates, such as Franklin Roosevelt, Lyndon Johnson, and Ronald Reagan, have enjoyed relatively smooth relations with Congress during their first terms, and used their broad popularity to achieve sweeping legislative successes—the New Deal, the Great Society, and a series of tax cuts dubbed "Reaganomics," respectively.

Other presidents, like Richard Nixon, Jimmy Carter, George H.W. Bush, and George W. Bush, either squandered their goodwill or lost the confidence of the people, and as a result were unable to accomplish much on the legislative front without bending to the will of Congress. It's no coincidence that Carter and George H.W. Bush were only one-term presidents.

The Courts

The Founding Fathers also vested Congress with broad authority to establish the federal court system. The Senate, in particular, was given the power to confirm judicial appointments. With that being the case, the Congress has been instrumental in shaping both the infrastructure of the court system and its ideological makeup.

The Congress also can influence the courts in more subtle ways. In the case of lawsuits brought against federal agencies, the courts will often interpret the "legislative intent" of the members in order to better understand the meaning of the federal statute at issue. Knowing this, legislators in both chambers have increasingly begun to leave vast paper trails explaining the meaning and intent of legislation passed by the Congress. In most cases, this legislative intent is mostly partisan spinning, and it tends to bear little resemblance to the actual intention of the statute. Nonetheless, courts are obliged to consider Congress's meaning when the plain language of the statute is unclear or ambiguous.

The Bureaucracy

One of the most important activities of Congress is overseeing the federal bureaucracy. It's up to Congress to ensure that the laws it passed are being properly administered and enforced. Members can hold committee and subcommittee hearings, conduct investigations, and subpoena documents to make this determination. Should something be amiss, Congress can force the bureaucracy into compliance by reducing the size of agency budgets or refusing to vote on key appointments. Members rely upon the Government Accountability Office (GAO) to help determine whether agencies are following the letter of the law.

THE ROLE OF STAFF

With members being pulled in a dozen different directions on any given day, staffers will often act as the "eyes and ears" for their bosses, doing everything from answering phones and reading mail to tending to constituent casework, monitoring legislative affairs, attending committee and subcommittee meetings, scheduling events, and communicating with the press.

Support Agencies

In addition to personal, office, and committee staffs, members of Congress have access to the expertise and knowledge of professional staffers at the Congressional Research Service (CRS), the Congressional Budget Office (CBO), and the Government Accountability Office (GAO), among others. These agencies were created for the express purpose of providing information to members of the House and Senate.

Over the past thirty years, the size of Congressional staff has grown dramatically (at taxpayer expense). As of 2009, more than 21,000 staffers worked in the district and Capitol offices of the members (though, to be fair, this number also includes staffers at bureaucratic agencies such as the GAO). Senators from the populous states receive a greater percentage of staff than those from less populous states, while House members all receive the same number of staff.

HOUSE VERSUS SENATE

Although early in the republic's history the House had greater prestige than the Senate, the balance between the chambers has shifted. This is largely owing to the change to direct election of senators, which began in 1913, and the growth of the House to its current size of 435 members. These days, it's very common for representatives to "graduate" to the Senate (almost a third of the current Senate has served in the House), while it's unheard of for a senator to seek a House seat. For politicians with national ambitions, the Senate has served as a viable steppingstone to the presidency and vice presidency. No sitting House representative has made it to either of these executive offices in more than seventy years.

Media Attention

For most House members not in a leadership position, getting the attention of the media is a full-time (and usually fruitless) task. Most reporters and broadcasters have little interest in covering the daily toiling of a representative unless it involves scandal or a gaffe.

Senators, on the other hand, are regulars on the six o'clock news and Sunday talk shows, particularly those from the larger states like California and New York, where they're thrust into the national spotlight simply by holding office. Even small-state and junior senators have little trouble getting media coverage on a regular basis.

This ability to garner media attention gives senators a national platform from which to advocate policy, raise money, increase their name recognition among the electorate, and lay the groundwork for a presidential campaign (should that be his or her ambition).

MAKING A LAW

Congress in Action

Have you ever wondered where our laws come from—who determines the amount of taxes we pay, the quality of our drinking water, the size of our social security check, or the laws and regulations governing our financial institutions? Most of us give it little thought because the process seems distant and complicated. The fact of the matter is, the way in which we, a self-governing people, create our laws is perhaps the most critical function of our government. We all share a stake in the outcome, and we should all be familiar with the process.

A NATION OF LAWS

The United States is a nation of laws. On a local, state, and national level, tens of thousands of laws are passed each year. Some are fairly innocuous, such as laws commemorating certain dates and events, while others have a profound impact on our daily lives. Laws can be broad or narrow, well known or obscure. Some laws have been around for decades, and others a few years.

Each year, thousands of bills are introduced in both chambers of Congress. Of these, only a fraction—a couple hundred at most—will make it to the president's desk for signature and become law. The rest are either quietly forgotten or rejected outright. The process of lawmaking is the central focus of the legislative branch, and its single most important duty.

Most of the legislation that is taken up by Congress involves mandatory issues: appropriations bills (those that determine which programs receive money) and authorization bills (those that allocate the amount of money for programs). Some matters are revisited every few years, such as increases in the minimum wage and revisions to the federal tax code. Other matters may be visited once every few decades. Incoming presidents typically have one or two high-profile pieces of legislation that make up the thrust of their domestic agenda, and those are typically given priority by the Congress.

The framers of the Constitution purposely established a framework whereby lawmaking would be difficult. To guard against an overreaching government, the framers created a lawmaking process that includes many opportunities for dissenters to derail legislation. As a consequence, only measures with broad appeal are able to survive this legislative gauntlet to become law.

INTRODUCING LEGISLATION

The first step to lawmaking is introducing a bill. Only a member of Congress can sponsor a bill, although inspiration for legislation can come from many different sources—the president, a lobbyist or interest group, a concerned citizen, or a constituency group in the district. Occasionally, members of the minority party will introduce legislation that they know has little chance of passing for the simple purpose of framing a policy position or scoring political points with the electorate.

Sometimes a member will draw from personal experience when sponsoring legislation. Such was the case for former Senator Strom Thurmond, who sponsored a bill requiring liquor companies to include warning labels in their print and broadcast advertising after his daughter was killed by a drunk driver. Former Senate Majority Leader Bob Dole helped establish National Men's Health Week after being diagnosed with prostate cancer.

On the Campaign Trail

After passage of the Affordable Care Act (dubbed "Obamacare") in 2010, Republican members of Congress railed against the new law. Republicans in the House voted at least sixty-seven times to repeal Obamacare. None of these attempts have been successful, but Republican candidates for president in 2016 made repealing the law a central part of their campaigns.

In most cases, the names of the sponsoring legislators are used as the informal name of the legislation, such as the Sarbanes-Oxley Act (for the Public Company Accounting Reform and Investor Protection Act of 2002).

Building Support and Drafting Legislation

Often, the sponsoring legislator will seek out fellow lawmakers to cosponsor his or her legislation as a way to demonstrate a broad base of support. On particularly high-profile bills, lawmakers will sometimes seek out members of the opposite party to cosponsor their legislation.

Although only members of Congress can introduce legislation, anyone can draft it. Most of the time, Congressional staff drafts legislation, though it's not uncommon for interest groups, activists, or the executive branch to put the words on paper. Many members take advantage of the attorneys and expert drafters at the nonpartisan Office of Legislative Counsel to help craft bills and amendments.

COMMITTEE REFERRAL

Once a bill has been introduced and drafted, it is assigned a number and referred to the appropriate committee for review. The proper committee is determined by the content of the bill; the committee most relevant to the subject matter receives jurisdiction.

In cases in which the subject matter is broad and encompasses several different areas, the legislation may be assigned to several committees for review. Securing a favorable committee for review—one that is likely to act on the legislation—can play a decisive role in the success or failure of the bill.

In very rare instances, the Speaker may bypass committee assignment altogether and send a bill directly to the House floor for review and vote. This is usually done when the Speaker wants to force a vote on a particularly controversial issue that is certain to embarrass the minority party.

COMMITTEE CONSIDERATION

The large majority of bills that are assigned to a committee languish without receiving any consideration and are quickly forgotten. For the few bills that are acted upon, the committee chairman will usually assign it to a subcommittee for further consideration. Subcommittees are where the bulk of legislative crafting takes place.

If the subcommittee decides to act, the first thing it does is hold hearings. Every year, Congressional committees and subcommittees hold thousands of hearings, with some receiving more attention than others. Hearings are held for several reasons:

- To explore the need for legislation
- To allow members to make their point of view known
- To build support and create a record for the legislation
- To attract media attention to the issue
- To give the chairman increased public exposure

The ranking members of the subcommittee call witnesses to testify on the pending legislation. This can include anyone from the sponsor of the bill to lobbyists, experts, other federal officials, ordinary citizens affected by the legislation, and even celebrities.

In most instances, the format doesn't vary much. Witnesses read a prepared statement, and then each subcommittee member is given an allotment of time (usually five minutes) to ask the witness questions. If the subcommittee chairman is opposed to the bill but doesn't want to publicly come out against it, he may hold an endless number of hearings as a way of slowly killing it without arousing suspicion among the public.

Committees and subcommittees are required by law to publish their hearing schedule a week in advance in local papers so that witnesses, the press, and the public are given appropriate time to prepare. While most hearings take place on Capitol Hill, sometimes committees conduct hearings in parts of the country where area residents will be particularly affected by the proposed legislation. It's not unusual for agriculture and dairy-related hearings to take place in Midwestern states, for example.

The Markup Phase

Once hearings have been completed, the bill enters the markup phase. During markup, subcommittee members debate the language of the bill, offer amendments, and vote on a final bill.

After markup, the bill is referred to the entire committee, where several things can occur. The committee may accept the recommendation, send it back to the subcommittee for further work, or conduct hearings and markups of its own. Usually, the committee accepts the findings of the subcommittee. Except for issues related to national security, committee and subcommittee markups must be conducted in public.

Report Submission

Once the bill has been written, the committee staff submits a report to all the members, explaining the contents of the bill. The committee report usually describes the purpose of the bill, contains the arguments for and against it, summarizes the hearing findings, explains how the bill may impact existing law, and includes a perspective from affected executive branch agencies. According to House and Senate rules, a majority of committee members must be present for a bill to be voted out of committee.

With a growing number of bills running into the thousands of pages (and written in confusing legalese), the report has become an invaluable tool for members to evaluate a piece of legislation. The courts and regulatory agencies that have to interpret and implement the law also rely upon the committee report to better understand the scope and meaning of the legislation. Committee members who oppose the final legislation are given the opportunity to file a supplemental report stating their views.

SCHEDULING DEBATE

Bills that are reported out of committee face one last obstacle before making it to the floor for debate and a vote: the calendar. Both the House and the Senate have specific calendars to determine the order in which bills are taken up by the entire chamber. In the House there are four different calendars, depending on the type of legislation:

1. The Union Calendar is reserved for bills that either raise or spend money.
2. The House Calendar is reserved for important public bills that do not deal with money.
3. The Private Calendar (or Consent Calendar) is reserved for noncontroversial items. (Here the formal rules are dispensed with so that items can be passed quickly.)
4. The Corrections Calendar is reserved for repealing frivolous or outdated laws and regulations that are still on the books.

The Senate has only two calendars:

1. The Executive Calendar is used to schedule confirmation proceedings for treaties and executive branch nominations.
2. The Calendar for General Orders is used to schedule all other matters (both public and private).

In the House, the Rules Committee controls the calendar; in the Senate, the majority and minority leaders set the schedule together.

FLOOR ACTION

The House Rules Committee announces the rules that govern the floor action of a bill. Like the other committees in Congress, the Rules Committee sometimes conducts hearings and calls witnesses when formulating a rule for a particular piece of legislation. The witnesses are usually members of the committee that is writing the bill.

In order for a House rule to take affect, it must be adopted by a majority of the chamber. If it fails to receive the requisite 218 votes, the Rules Committee can either turn to another rule or let the bill die in committee. Before the vote takes place, the Speaker usually allots one hour of debate between the majority and minority members of the Rules Committee, with the ranking members acting as floor managers.

Once in a while, either a standing committee will refuse to report on a bill or it will not be granted a rule from the Rules Committee. In those situations, members can file a petition to discharge the bill from committee and bring it directly to the floor. The rarely used discharge petition can be filed by any member, and requires a majority of signatures. In cases in which a member is secretly opposed to a particular piece of legislation but is hesitant to vote against it for fear of rousing public anger, he can vote against the rule (and thus defeat the bill) without being on the record as having voted against the bill itself.

Debate and Amendments

Once a bill receives its rule, it goes to the floor for debate and amendment. In both the Senate and the House, floor managers—

usually the chairman and ranking minority member of the committee that wrote the bill—are appointed to "quarterback" this process. The majority floor manager tries to shepherd the bill to final passage, while the minority floor manager tries to defeat it.

The debate and amendment process play different roles in the two chambers. In the House, debate is almost always perfunctory. It mostly serves as an opportunity for members to make their viewpoints known to the public and in some cases grandstand on the issue.

In the Senate, however, legislation takes its shape on the floor. Senators take advantage of the unlimited debate and amendments to add and subtract provisions, negotiate concessions, and alter language of the final bill.

Time to Take a Vote

As soon as debate has ended, the bill comes to a final vote. They have one of three options to select from: Yes, No, or Present. Present is used when a member doesn't want to be on record against a particular bill, but he doesn't want to support it either. Members have fifteen minutes to vote, and an electronic bulletin board near the press gallery keeps a running tally of "yeas" and "nays."

AGREEMENT BETWEEN THE HOUSE AND SENATE

Before a bill can be forwarded to the president, the House and Senate versions must be identical. Most of the time, this is not an issue, because the two chambers usually coordinate the wording of the legislation throughout the process. About a quarter of the time, however, the House and Senate bills contain different provisions. On these occasions, a conference committee is needed to reconcile the gaps.

During conference committees, representatives from both chambers work to iron out the language differences between the two bills. The chairman and ranking minority member of the committee with jurisdiction select the conferees from their respective chambers. The number of conferees depends on the size and complexity of the two bills. The ratio of Republicans and Democrats chosen as conferees usually mirrors the ratio between the two parties in the House and Senate.

Once the conferees have come to agreement over a compromise bill, it is presented to and voted on by both chambers. On the rare occasions when one or both bodies reject the new bill, another conference can be convened, or the bill can be shelved. If the bill is passed by both chambers, it is sent to the president.

PRESIDENTIAL PREROGATIVE

The final leg of the legislative journey is the White House, where the president can either sign the bill into law or veto it. But even if the president rejects the legislation, Congress still has one final recourse—it can override the president's veto with a two-thirds vote of both chambers. This process, however, is extremely difficult and rare, so much so that less than 5 percent of all presidential vetoes have been overridden. Nevertheless, the ability to override a veto remains one of Congress's most important checks over the presidency.

CREATING A BUDGET

Raising and Spending Money

Deciding how much the government is going to spend in a fiscal year and what it's going to spend the money on is one of the most contentious of all Congressional deliberations. Part of this is because the sums are so huge; in 2015 the federal government spent a staggering $3.688 trillion. This money was for programs ranging from the space program and national defense to the national endowments for the arts and humanities, Social Security, Medicare, interstate highway construction, and even midnight basketball.

Another reason the issue is argued about so much is that each party has spending priorities, and individual congresspersons and senators are anxious to direct federal dollars to their own district or state.

CONTROL OVER THE FEDERAL BUDGET

The Constitution gives Congress the power to raise funds (tax) and appropriate (spend money). The framers believed that the enormous power of taxing and spending was best left to the Congress, because it was feared that the president could abuse the power to serve his own ends and perhaps even overthrow the government. The theory was that Congress could check the power of the presidency by controlling the resources at his disposal.

Article I, Section 8 of the Constitution provides only four general guidelines for federal spending:

1. All money drawn from the treasury must result from an appropriations bill.
2. Congress must account for all expenditures from "time to time."
3. Appropriations that support the military expire after two years.
4. All expenditures must be made for the "general welfare" of the United States.

The Constitution says all spending bills must originate in the House of Representatives and then be sent to the Senate once the House has completed its work. Today, though, they may be introduced simultaneously in both chambers.

On the Campaign Trail

A major issue in the midterm elections of 2010 were the Bush tax cuts—a series of tax reductions enacted during the administration of George W. Bush. Critics of the cuts, which were due to expire in 2010 unless Congress enacted legislation to save them, claimed the cuts increased both the budget deficit and income inequality. After a bruising debate during the election, Republicans and Democrats hammered out an agreement to extend the tax cuts by two years. Many of them were later extended indefinitely.

In 1921 Congress passed the Budget and Accounting Act. The act gave the president a formal role in the process, requiring him to submit an annual budget to Congress. It also barred federal agencies from making appropriations requests directly to Congress, and established the Bureau of the Budget (renamed the Office of Management and Budget in 1970) to help the president set his budget.

The Congressional Budget and Impoundment Control Act of 1974, which President Nixon signed into law just a month before resigning from office, called for Congress to adopt its own budget resolution, as well as set revenue and spending goals. It also established the Congressional Budget Office (CBO), which provides Congress with its own economic assumptions, program analysis, and budget recommendations.

Thanks to the passage of the 1974 act, Congress and the president have an equal role in the budget process. However, because of that equality, the process became—and remains—acrimonious, partisan, and excruciatingly deliberate.

BUDGETARY OVERSIGHT

Hammering Out a Spending Bill

Congress's most effective oversight tool is the authorization and appropriations process. When an agency is established, Congress must authorize funds for it. In some cases, such as the Social Security Administration (SSA), this is a permanent authorization, meaning it never has to be renewed. For others, such as NASA, this authorization is periodic—it must be renewed every few years. In light of this, Congress wields much greater control over agencies that require periodic authorizations.

Congress also controls the annual budgets for both permanently and periodically authorized agencies through the appropriations process. This gives Congress the ability to abolish or modify agency programs by eliminating or cutting back funding. Agency heads periodically testify before the Congressional committees and subcommittees with jurisdiction to request funding increases.

DEFICITS AND DEBTS

Since the early twentieth century, the budget process has been characterized by annual deficits and mounting public debt. Deficits occur when government spending exceeds revenues (that is, the amount of money that it takes in). Since revenues and spending goals are estimated a year in advance of their enactment, these figures are frequently incorrect.

Sometimes the government will purposely "deficit spend" in order to prevent the economy from going into recession or to bring it out of one. In 2008 during the Great Recession, the Troubled Asset Relief Program (TARP) spent $431 billion to prop up elements of the U.S. economy.

Public (or national) debt is the accumulation of years of deficits. As of the beginning of 2016, the gross national debt was approximately $19 trillion. Every year, one of the largest government expenditures—more than $200 billion—goes toward paying interest on the national debt.

RAISING REVENUES

Revenue is the money that the government collects from taxes, fees, borrowing, and other sources. Before 1913, when the Sixteenth Amendment was passed, Congress didn't have the power to enact an income tax. Before then, the federal government's chief revenue sources had been tariffs and excise taxes. Things have changed quite dramatically since then. In 2014, approximately 46 percent of all revenues came from individual income taxes, while nearly 34 percent came from Social Security (payroll) taxes, 10.6 percent from corporate taxes, 3.1 percent from excise taxes, and 6.3 percent from other sources.

The payroll tax is deducted directly from wages and salaries in order to pay for Social Security, Medicare, unemployment insurance, and disability insurance. Both employers and employees contribute to these programs (self-employed individuals pay both parts of the tax).

THE AMERICAN PRESIDENT

The Most Powerful Person in the World

The U.S. presidency is arguably the most powerful office in the world, and the most coveted job in America. Although the Constitution established the Congress as the first branch of government, the presidency has supplanted it as the focal point of our system over the course of 200 years.

The presidency and the vice presidency are the only nationally elected offices, which means that the president enjoys a mandate unlike any other in American politics. It's also the only term-limited position among the three branches of government. And the president serves as both chief executive and head of state.

But what makes the presidency truly special is that the office is greater than the sum of its constitutional parts. The person who occupies the White House is more than just the commander in chief, chief executive, chief legislator, chief diplomat, and head of state. The president represents America abroad and the aspirations of Americans at home. World economic markets react to his actions and utterances. He is the leader of the free world and commander of the lone superpower. The president speaks to the people and embodies our values. He alone can comfort a nation in mourning, lead us during times of crises, and rally us to war and peace. And only the president can command the nation's attention with a single speech or comment.

We ask a lot of the president and vice president as candidates, and we demand even more of them in office. We place in them our trust and hope that it is rewarded. Whether we voted for the president or not, we expect him to be the president of all the people.

THE FIRST AMERICAN PRESIDENT

George Washington, the father of our country, understood that every action he took while president would establish a precedent for future officeholders, and he kept that in mind throughout his eight years in the White House. He wanted to make certain that future presidents acted with humility and respected the separation of powers among the three branches of government.

Perhaps Washington's most important precedent was to walk away from the office after two terms. It's hard to imagine it now, but at the time it was an extraordinary notion for the head of a nation-state to voluntarily turn over the seat of government to someone else and retire.

His Highness the President?

As George Washington's vice president, John Adams spent a good deal of time trying to figure out how the president should be formally addressed. He was in favor of an elegant title, and proposed "His Highness the President, Protector of the Liberties of the United States" to the Senate. Thankfully, Washington settled on "Mr. President."

Washington also believed that the president should seek the best available minds for his cabinet, even if they didn't agree on every issue. His cabinet included Thomas Jefferson, Alexander Hamilton, and Edmund Randolph, three giants of the day who held different political philosophies.

George Washington shaped the office in other ways as well:

- He successfully asserted the right to remove his cabinet officers without Senate approval.
- He established the president's supremacy in organizing the executive branch.
- He used the veto power very sparingly, believing it was important not to usurp the will of the people.
- He asserted presidential control during times of emergency when he nationalized state militias to put down the Whiskey Rebellion.
- He made a point of touring all corners of the country so that the American people could meet the president.

EVOLUTION OF THE PRESIDENCY

More than any other branch of government, the presidency has undergone a remarkable transformation during the past 200-plus years. Though the framers did not provide the presidency with many powers, and George Washington tried to keep it that way, the balance of power between the presidency and Congress shifted over the decades.

The Era of the Caretaker Presidents

The nineteenth century was the era of great legislators, not presidents. The initial wave of founding father presidents (Washington, Adams, Jefferson, and Madison) quickly gave way to a collection of relatively weak and forgettable officeholders.

The presidency was looked upon mostly as a source of federal patronage jobs, and a platform from which to fight the Indians. In fact, the president spent much of his time actually interviewing and appointing thousands of federal workers, which included mail carriers, census officials, and patent reviewers. The dominant issues of the day—slavery and states' rights—were debated in Congress. However, two presidents from this era do stand out: Andrew Jackson and Abraham Lincoln.

Andrew Jackson

"Old Hickory" believed that the presidency should be the dominant force in American government. He asserted the right of the president to replace any federal officeholder without consulting Congress, and wasn't shy about putting his cronies in key government positions (thus creating the patronage system). He stood up to the members of Congress who opposed tariffs, and he threatened to use the military to enforce federal law.

Abraham Lincoln

Regarded by many as our greatest president, Lincoln's election led to secession of the Confederate states from the union. Faced with the greatest crisis the country had encountered up to that point (and arguably since), Lincoln understood that only the president could keep the country together. Citing the implied emergency powers of the Constitution, he freed the slaves, suspended civil liberties, and imposed marshal law, even though he lacked the explicit authority to do so. His most important act, however, may have been his decision to hold the election of 1864 during the midst of the Civil War, even though he probably could have suspended it.

The Modern Presidency

The modern presidency bears little resemblance to its nineteenth-century antecedent. As the federal government has grown in size and influence, so has the presidency. Since the beginning of the twentieth century, the president has become the dominant force in American government and politics. This seemingly irreversible trend was pioneered by some of the twentieth century's most prominent presidents.

Teddy Roosevelt

Theodore Roosevelt established the notion of the "bully pulpit"—using the prestige and reach of the White House to rally the American people to certain ideas and legislation. Roosevelt believed that America should pursue an expansionist foreign policy and a populist domestic policy.

Franklin Roosevelt

FDR responded to the challenge of the Great Depression with the New Deal, a series of landmark laws that transformed the role of the federal government and solidified the presidency as the epicenter of American government. During his thirteen years in office, Roosevelt dramatically expanded the powers of the presidency to combat the Great Depression and wage war against Germany and Japan. By the end of World War II, the presidency was a much stronger office than the one that Roosevelt had inherited.

The Cold War Presidents

The cold war between the United States and the Soviet Union may have done more to enhance the powers of the presidency than any single event during the twentieth century. America's role in the world became the primary preoccupation of the president, and consequently spurred an unprecedented growth of the executive branch and presidential powers. While the Congress remained instrumental in domestic affairs, it acquiesced to the president on matters of foreign policy and war powers.

PRESIDENTIAL DUTIES

A Day in the Life of the Chief Executive

The presidency is a 24/7 occupation. Regardless of whether he's enjoying a weekend at Camp David, spending some quiet time in the residential quarters, or simply vacationing, the president is always the president of the United States. He can be pressed into action at a moment's notice. At no time is he free from the duties of the job.

The president's daily routine is usually packed with meetings, events, briefings, speeches, and public ceremonies. His time and schedule are highly regimented and closely guarded by his chief of staff. The activities of a typical day may include:

- Receiving security briefings from heads of the FBI, CIA, NSA, and the Department of Homeland Security
- Making phone calls to other heads of state
- Meeting with members of Congress
- Meeting with governors and other state officials
- Meeting with cabinet officials and other executive agency personnel
- Having lunch with the vice president
- Attending public events and ceremonies
- Discussing policy with advisers and staff
- Speaking with the media
- Making public remarks from the White House
- Signing bills and executive orders into law
- Attending fundraisers or other political events
- Traveling on behalf of candidates

During the past fifty years, presidential travel—both domestic and international—has increased sharply. The president typically spends two months of every year in domestic travel, and another twenty days outside of the country. Travel at home is used primarily to boost the president's standing in certain regions of the country, and usually peaks around the midterm elections. The president travels overseas to meet with foreign heads of state, attend conferences and summits with world leaders, and rally the American troops during times of conflict.

STYLES OF LEADERSHIP

Each president who occupies the White House brings his own style of leadership to the position. Political scientists have theorized that leadership style is an indicator of how a president will organize his administration and approach the job.

Delegators

Presidents Franklin D. Roosevelt and Ronald Reagan are considered examples of delegators. Both brought a broad, bold vision of the role of government to the White House, and each relied heavily upon staff, executive agencies, and cabinet heads to implement their policies.

Micromanagers

Presidents Lyndon B. Johnson and Jimmy Carter were known as micromanagers. As a former Senate majority leader, Johnson took an unusually active role in Congressional affairs, and was fond of monitoring the minutiae of the legislative process. He took a similar approach to managing the Vietnam War, picking many of the bombing targets himself during late-night strategy sessions with his generals.

Charismatic Leaders

Presidents John F. Kennedy and Bill Clinton are regarded as charismatic leaders—extraordinary communicators who used the media to project an image of youth, vitality, and action. Both presidents drew heavily from academia to fill high-profile positions and were persuasive advocates for their agendas.

WHO RUNS?

Running for president of the United States, in the words of one political analyst, requires someone with a big enough ego to think that he should be president of the United States and the humility to appreciate the responsibilities of the office. There are three constitutional requirements for becoming president: The candidate must be a natural-born citizen of the United States, have been a resident of the country for the fourteen years prior, and be at least thirty-five years old.

On the Campaign Trail

During Barack Obama's administration, a group of opponents dubbed "birthers" insisted against all evidence that the president was born in Kenya instead of Hawaii. They insisted this made him ineligible to serve. (The president released his birth certificate, showing clearly that he was born in Honolulu.) Similar questions were raised in the 2016 campaign about Senator Ted Cruz, who really was born in Canada. Prevailing legal opinion is that since his mother is an American, he is a "natural-born" citizen.

Different Paths

Just as the office has evolved over the past 200 years, so has the typical route to the White House. Throughout the nineteenth century, a large majority of presidents (and candidates who lost the elections) were either generals or senators. Only a few were governors, and even fewer were businessmen. The past 100 years have seen a dramatic reversal: Dwight D. Eisenhower has been the only general to serve as president, and governors have outnumbered senators.

PRESIDENTIAL SUCCESSION

Who Comes Next?

The wording of the Constitution is somewhat ambiguous when it comes to the subject of replacing the president. All it says is, "In Case of the Removal of the President from Office, or of his Death, Resignation, or Inability to discharge the Powers and Duties of the said Office, the Same shall devolve on the Vice President."

When William Henry Harrison became the first president to die in office, in 1841, no one was sure whether Vice President John Tyler would become president or whether he would simply be entrusted with discharging the duties of the presidential office. Many in Congress considered Tyler to be the "acting president," although Tyler himself behaved as though he were the president. Tyler's approach won the day, and he established the precedent that the vice president was to be elevated to president upon the president's death or removal from office.

The President with the Briefest Term

William Henry Harrison was the first president to die in office and remains the president with the shortest tenure, serving only thirty-one days. Harrison caught a severe case of pneumonia while delivering a three-hour inaugural speech in freezing weather.

What happens if both the president and vice president die at the same time? The Presidential Succession Act of 1947, passed by President Harry S. Truman, established the order of succession should both officials die, resign, or become incapacitated. The Speaker of the House is next in line, followed by the president pro tempore of the Senate. After that, it falls to the cabinet officers according to the order in which their departments were created:

1. Secretary of State
2. Secretary of the Treasury
3. Secretary of Defense
4. Attorney General
5. Secretary of the Interior
6. Secretary of Agriculture
7. Secretary of Commerce
8. Secretary of Labor
9. Secretary of Health and Human Services
10. Secretary of Housing and Urban Development
11. Secretary of Transportation
12. Secretary of Energy
13. Secretary of Education
14. Secretary of Veterans Affairs
15. Secretary of Homeland Security

THE POWERS OF THE PRESIDENT

What Can the Chief Executive Do?

As chief executive, the president has the authority to enforce the laws of the country. The president has at his disposal the entire executive branch (almost 4 million workers) to help carry out the laws of the land. Additionally, the president has the power of appointments and pardons.

MAKING APPOINTMENTS

While the president exercises the power to make judicial and executive branch appointments, the Senate must approve his nominees. This process has grown increasingly contentious over the past few decades, particularly in the case of cabinet and Supreme Court appointments.

On the Campaign Trail

The president's ability to nominate justices to the Supreme Court became an issue in the 2016 election when, after the death of conservative Justice Antonin Scalia, Senate Majority Leader Mitch McConnell declared the Senate would not consider anyone nominated by President Obama because the country was in an election year. The new justice, he said, should be nominated by whoever was elected president in November.

Out of the 4 million federal jobs, most are held by civil servants who are hired, but approximately 6,000 are appointed by the executive branch.

While a majority of the executive branch appointments are made on the basis of merit, some are given to reward party loyalists, and others are made for purely political reasons. Most presidents treat ambassadorships as nothing more than thank-you appointments to prominent campaign and party donors. For cabinet and other high-profile appointments, the president usually takes into consideration those nominees who will shore up their support with certain interest groups.

"Every time I make an appointment, I create nine enemies and one ingrate."

—Thomas Jefferson

GRANTING PARDONS

The Constitution gives the president the power to "grant Reprieves and Pardons for Offences against the United States, except in Cases of Impeachment." The ability to grant pardons and reprieves is one of the few constitutional powers of the presidency that does not require any assent from the Congress.

A reprieve is an action whereby the president can reduce the severity or length of a felon's sentence, but it does not erase the conviction. A pardon, on the other hand, wipes out both the guilt and sentence, and completely restores all civil rights to the offender.

Perhaps the most famous act of clemency was Gerald Ford's pardon of Richard Nixon following Nixon's resignation from office in 1974. Trying to put the Watergate scandal behind the nation, Ford granted his predecessor a full and unconditional pardon, which removed the possibility of Nixon being prosecuted in a criminal court for his involvement in any Watergate crimes.

HEAD OF STATE

In countries like Great Britain, Sweden, Denmark, and Belgium, the king or queen serves as the head of state, while an elected prime minister or president discharges the chief executive functions. Other countries, such as France, Italy, and Germany, have an elected head of state (usually a president) who works alongside an elected chief executive (usually a prime minster). In the United States, the president serves both of these functions—a rarity among Western democracies.

The president is a symbol of our government and the nation. He represents the majesty and dignity of the office both at home and abroad, and provides our national voice. His gestures—no matter how big or small—carry special meaning and importance. It was reported that the sale of hats dropped dramatically following John F. Kennedy's inauguration, because the president broke with tradition and failed to don one during the parade. When Jimmy Carter turned the White House thermostat down to sixty-five degrees in the winter to save energy, the nation followed suit.

COMMANDER IN CHIEF

Over the years, presidents have exercised more authority in their role as commander in chief than in any other facet of the job. It's without question the most important responsibility of the office. As commander in chief, the president has the ability to commit American troops to battle. It is the most difficult decision a president can make, and is always handled with great care and reflection.

Declaring War

The framers of the Constitution were careful not to vest too much military power in the presidency for fear of creating an abusive and unjust government, or even a military dictatorship. Therefore, the Constitution gives the Congress the authority to declare war, raise an army, and fund wars, while it gives the president the power to manage and execute military action. The framers did not want the president to have the ability to both declare and execute wars without Congressional involvement.

For the most part, nineteenth-century presidents adhered to the Constitution when it came to decisions of war, consulting Congress on military actions and committing troops only with formal declarations of war. Preceding both World War I and World War II, however, the Congress delegated by statute to the president increased authority to fight wars. The onset of the cold war with the Soviet Union resulted in even greater military authority for the president.

The Korean War was the first large-scale war for which the president did not seek prior Congressional approval. Harry Truman cited the commander-in-chief authority as well as a United Nations resolution authorizing the use of force as justification for sending troops into battle without a formal declaration of war. Ten years later, President Lyndon Johnson relied on this precedent to send troops to Vietnam—another undeclared war.

In response to the Vietnam War, the Congress passed the War Powers Act in 1973 over President Richard Nixon's veto. With this act, the Congress tried to reign in the president's ability to make war, setting out a specific set of conditions under which he could commit troops without prior Congressional authorization. Even though the Supreme Court has struck down parts of the act as unconstitutional, it has been somewhat successful in forcing presidents to seek Congressional approval before sending troops into harm's way.

Military Commander

As part of his commander-in-chief function, the president is in charge of the armed forces—he is the first general and admiral. Presidents have approached the military commander function differently. Depending on their background, some have taken a more hands-on approach, while others have left all the decision-making up to their generals. In 1794, George Washington nearly took charge of the militia that put down the Whiskey Rebellion. During the Civil War, Abraham Lincoln was deeply involved in strategy, troop movements, and battle plans, and on occasion even gave direct orders to his field generals. President Woodrow Wilson left the battlefield strategy to the military during World War I, as did President Franklin Roosevelt (for the most part) in World War II. Lyndon Johnson was famous for selecting specific bombing targets in Vietnam. In the wars in Iraq and Afghanistan, both George W. Bush and Barack Obama have largely left military tactics to their generals.

The Nuclear Football

Wherever the president goes, a military aide follows him carrying "the football"—a briefcase containing all the codes and documents necessary to order a nuclear launch. The president is the only person with the power to authorize a nuclear launch.

CHIEF DIPLOMAT

The president needs the consent of two-thirds of the Senate in order to enter into a foreign treaty. Some presidents have interpreted this to mean that the Senate should be consulted on all aspects of treaty negotiations, while others have viewed Senate approval as a rubber stamp.

Regardless of interpretation, the president is the one who drives the treaty process. He alone decides which treaties to pursue. He selects the negotiators, devises the negotiating strategy, and lobbies the Senate for approval. He can even reject a treaty that the Senate has approved if he doesn't like the changes made to it. A treaty is not officially recognized until the president signs it into law.

Although the president needs the Senate's consent to ratify a treaty, he does not need it to terminate one. The Constitution is silent on this issue, but the Supreme Court has held that the president alone should have the power to terminate treaties.

Executive Agreements

An executive agreement is a pact between the United States and a foreign government that falls short of being a treaty but binds the two countries to a mutual action. Such pacts include arms reduction promises, trade agreements, military commitments, and territory annexation plans. An executive agreement is a powerful foreign policy tool because it does not require Senate approval and because it gives the president the flexibility to negotiate international agreements quickly and in secret—two important considerations when dealing with sensitive and timely matters.

The biggest difference between treaties and executive agreements is that treaties are binding on all future presidents, while executive agreements must be reauthorized by each succeeding administration. Executive agreements have grown increasingly popular over the past five decades. In total, there have been more than 15,000 executive agreements, compared to 1,900 treaties.

Diplomatic Recognition

Although it's not an explicit power in the Constitution, the president also has the sole authority to recognize a foreign government. Formal recognition of a foreign government is required before treaties, executive agreements, and other diplomatic actions can take place. The simple act of receiving a foreign diplomat is enough to officially recognize his or her government.

In some cases, presidents have used the recognition power to make a political statement. President Andrew Jackson recognized the independent country of Texas in 1836 because he knew it would provoke Mexico into a war with the United States. Harry Truman recognized the newly created state of Israel in 1946 as a way to support the fledgling country. In 1978, Jimmy Carter recognized the Palestinian Authority in Israeli-occupied territories in an effort to jump-start the peace process. President Clinton severed relations with Afghanistan after the Taliban seized power, and President

George W. Bush reinstated it after the provisional government of Hamid Karzai took control. President Barack Obama, in 2016, made a historic visit to Cuba, the first president to do so since the Cuban Revolution in 1959.

LEGISLATOR IN CHIEF

The president plays a dominant role in the legislative process. He proposes legislation, works closely with Congressional leadership on scheduling and strategy, and frequently lobbies members on key votes. When the president is of the same party as the Congressional majority, his legislative agenda is given top priority.

State of the Union Address

This annual State of the Union address has developed into the president's most powerful tool to shape the legislative agenda. For most of the nineteenth century, presidents discharged this responsibility with a letter to Congress. Beginning with Woodrow Wilson, however, the president began delivering the State of the Union address in person. It is now given in late January to a packed session of Congress (including the Supreme Court justices and cabinet officials). The nationally televised address allows the president to lay out a comprehensive legislative agenda for the coming session of Congress.

Veto Power

The Constitution vests the president with the power to veto—or reject—any legislation passed by the Congress. This power is a valuable political tool because it allows the president to influence and shape legislation simply by raising the specter of a veto.

Presidents tend to exercise the veto power judiciously. Using it too often can give the appearance of being out of touch with the American people, or behaving like an obstructionist.

PARTY LEADER

The president's most important political party function is fundraising. Every year, the president raises hundreds of millions of dollars for his party and fellow officeholders at the state and national level. Cabinet members and high-profile White House officials assist in the fundraising, particularly during election seasons. During the 1990s, many Republicans, consumer advocate groups, and even some in the press criticized President Clinton for his aggressive use of the White House for political party fundraising.

In addition to fundraising, the president also has the following responsibilities as the leader of his party:

- He selects the national committee chairperson.
- He appoints thousands of individuals to White House, executive agency, and quasi-government positions.
- He writes the party policy platform at the nominating convention.
- He influences party members in Congress with promises of fundraising support and projects for their district.
- He campaigns for candidates.

IMPEACHMENT

Removing the President

There are only three ways a president can leave office during his term:

1. He can die in office.
2. He can resign.
3. He can be impeached, convicted, and removed.

The Constitution lays out the process of impeachment, a procedure that can be applied to other federal officials (for example, judges) as well. In its essence, impeachment and trial of a president are straightforward.

The House of Representatives—and only the House—has the power to impeach elected officials. The framers considered impeachment to be one of the most potent checks in American government. They believed that it should only be used sparingly, and with the consent of the people.

The president, according to the Constitution, can be impeached for "Treason, Bribery, or other high Crimes and Misdemeanors." However, since the document doesn't make clear what these are, it is up to the House to determine the grounds for impeachment. Members of the House can introduce a bill calling for the impeachment of the president or they can refer action to a committee. If a majority of that committee believe impeachment should move forward, they will report out the bill (return the bill after consideration) calling for impeachment on specific grounds.

The articles of impeachment then go before the entire House, where they are debated and voted upon. If they are approved by a majority, they are sent to the Senate, which conducts a trial.

TRIAL BY SENATE

While the House of Representatives has the sole ability to impeach federal officials, the Senate has exclusive domain over trial and conviction. Impeachment trials have been held only sixteen times in Senate history, with the result being seven convictions, seven acquittals, and two officials stepping down before the proceedings concluded. All seven convicted officials were federal judges. No president has ever been removed from office. Richard Nixon would have been the first president convicted by the Senate had he not resigned in August of 1974.

In 1805, the Senate established the precedent that impeachment would not be used for political retribution when it acquitted Supreme Court Justice Samuel Chase, an outspoken Federalist and vocal critic of the Jefferson administration. Nearly 200 years later, a similar controversy was revisited when President Clinton was impeached for allegedly perjuring himself before a grand jury. Given the Constitution's vague language about what constitutes an impeachable offense, there was fierce disagreement over the propriety of Clinton's impeachment and trial.

Most scholars and commentators took the position that conviction and removal should be reserved for indictable crimes only, while some took a broader interpretation and sought to use it as a political weapon. The narrow viewpoint won the day, as President Clinton was easily acquitted of both counts.

Despite the fact that no president has ever been impeached and convicted and removed from office, impeachment remains a potent weapon in the hands of Congress.

THE FIRST LADY

An Evolving Role

Although there is no mention of the role of first lady in the Constitution, it has developed into an important position in American government. After all, perhaps no other person carries as much influence with the president as his spouse.

FIRST LADIES AND THEIR CAUSES

Whereas first ladies were once confined to simply setting the social calendar and hosting White House receptions, today they work on issues of public policy and advance agendas based on their own interests. Recent first ladies have adopted the following causes:

- Jacqueline Kennedy devoted herself to restoring the White House and establishing the White House Historical Association.
- Lady Bird Johnson continued Jacqueline Kennedy's work, creating the First Ladies Commission for a More Beautiful Capital.
- Pat Nixon enhanced the White House art collection and was a strong proponent of volunteerism.
- Betty Ford was closely identified with her fight against drug and alcohol abuse, and founded the Betty Ford Center.
- Rosalynn Carter worked with the mentally ill, and served as the honorary chairwoman of the President's Commission on Mental Health.
- Nancy Reagan started the "Just Say No" campaign, an antidrug and antialcohol program targeted at young Americans.

- Barbara Bush focused on adult literacy and elderly care.
- Hillary Rodham Clinton took an active role in public policy, serving as chairwoman of the National Commission on Health Care Reform. She was also an advocate for children, and author of the bestselling book *It Takes a Village*.
- Laura Bush, like her mother-in-law, promoted literacy. She also played an important role in comforting parents and children across the country in the weeks and months following the terrorist attacks of September 11, 2001.
- Michelle Obama took up the cause of obesity among children and advocated for a healthier diet at home and in schools.

THREE WHO STOOD OUT

Of the thirty-eight women who have occupied the White House as first ladies, three in particular have stood out for their achievements. These women were instrumental in shaping the role of the first lady.

Eleanor Roosevelt

Eleanor Roosevelt revolutionized the role of first lady, transforming it from hostess to public policy advocate. She was a tireless advocate for the poor and underprivileged, reaching out to millions through barnstorming tours, a weekly newspaper column, press conferences, and frequent radio interviews. After leaving the White House, Eleanor Roosevelt carried on her husband's legacy of social activism and also served as the United States ambassador to the United Nations.

Jacqueline Kennedy

Perhaps more than any first lady before or since, Jacqueline Kennedy is responsible for restoring the beauty and elegance of the White House. Her interest in the arts, culture, and the history of the White House captured the imagination of the country, and added to the youthful and energetic image of her husband's administration. Jacqueline Kennedy won the admiration of the world for her strength and courage following the assassination of President Kennedy.

Hillary Rodham Clinton

Eleanor Roosevelt began the transformation of the role of first lady, and Hillary Rodham Clinton completed it, elevating the role of public policy advocate to the primary responsibility of the first lady. Like Eleanor Roosevelt, her public service did not end after leaving the White House. As the junior senator from New York, she is the only first lady to hold elected office. Hillary Clinton blazed a new path for women in politics through her roles as first lady, U.S. senator, secretary of state, and as a candidate for the presidency in 2008 and 2016.

THE VICE PRESIDENT

Ready to Serve

The vice presidency is a peculiar office. It has virtually no constitutional authority, and has often been relegated to an afterthought by the president. Yet the person who occupies it is only a heartbeat away from assuming the presidency. For the first 150 years, the vice president played almost no role in American government. Since World War II, however, the vice presidency has assumed greater responsibilities, and very recently has blossomed into the second most powerful position in Washington. It has been a strange journey for the office that has been described as the "president's understudy."

"The man with the best job in the country is the vice president. All he has to do is get up every morning and say, 'How is the president?'"

—Will Rogers

THE EARLY YEARS

The vice presidency was given little consideration by the framers of the Constitution. Some of them were opposed to having the position at all, so as a compromise it was made into a weak office. A last-minute insertion into the Constitution gave it just one explicit duty—to preside over the Senate.

The country's first constitutional crisis occurred during the election of 1800, when Thomas Jefferson and Aaron Burr received the same number of presidential votes in the Electoral College. What made it particularly troublesome was that Burr was Jefferson's running mate!

The Constitution set up a system in which there was no separate vote for president and vice president. Members of the Electoral College were allowed to submit two votes, but they could not indicate which vote was for president and which was for vice president. The candidate receiving the most votes was elected president, and the runner-up was made vice president. The framers created this odd system because they wanted the vice president to be the second most qualified person in the country.

What the system didn't anticipate were political parties and running mates. In the election of 1800, Jefferson and his running mate Burr both received 73 electoral votes, while Jefferson's opponent John Adams received only 65. By constitutional mandate, the election was then thrown to the House of Representatives, where on the thirty-sixth ballot Jefferson finally edged out his vice presidential running mate.

On the Campaign Trail

As the presidential election was being contested in the House of Representatives, Alexander Hamilton worked behind the scenes to deny Aaron Burr a victory. Hamilton detested Burr, and thought he was unfit for the office. Burr blamed Hamilton for his defeat, and four years later (while serving as vice president) challenged Hamilton to a duel, during which Burr shot and killed him.

As a result of the mess of 1800, the Twelfth Amendment was passed, which called for separate ballots for the election of the president and vice president. Thus, instead of the second most qualified person obtaining the office of vice president (the presidential loser), the president's running mate would become the vice president.

The Veeps That History Forgot

Few men of national stature were interested in the powerless office, and as a result a rash of vastly underqualified candidates filled the void. Garret Hobart was a New Jersey state legislator when he was tapped as William McKinley's vice president. Chester Arthur, who became president after James Garfield was assassinated, had been a customs collector for the port of New York prior to becoming vice president.

THE MODERN VICE PRESIDENCY

The presidency of Dwight Eisenhower marked a turning point for the vice presidency. "I personally believe the Vice President of the United States should never be a nonentity. I believe he should be used. I believe he should have a very useful job," Ike once remarked at a press conference.

Eisenhower lived up to those words, giving his number-two man Richard Nixon a more prominent role than any previous vice president. Nixon served as the party spokesperson and political trouble-shooter, and was active in foreign affairs. He traveled to fifty-eight nations—far and away the most of any previous vice president—and conducted several sensitive diplomatic missions on Ike's behalf.

Lyndon Johnson picked up on Nixon's role as goodwill ambassador to the world. Johnson too went globetrotting to meet with foreign heads of state on dozens of occasions. As a former Senate majority leader, he played a part in devising the Kennedy administration's legislative strategy—particularly for the civil rights bill—and was also given broad responsibilities with the newly created National Aeronautics and Space Administration (NASA). Johnson's time as vice president prepared him well for assuming the presidency following President Kennedy's assassination in November of 1963.

Spiro Agnew's tenure as Richard Nixon's vice president represented something of a setback for the office. Agnew is best remembered for his scathing attacks against the news media and the "elite establishment," and for resigning the office in disgrace after pleading nolo contendere to the charge of income tax evasion.

Al Gore and Dick Cheney

Since the early 1990s, the vice presidency has taken another leap forward in stature and importance. During that time, it has completed the transition from an office of ridicule to one of the most powerful positions in Washington. Former presidents Bill Clinton and George W. Bush are largely responsible for this final metamorphosis, having given their vice presidents more responsibility than did any previous administration.

VICE PRESIDENT AS SUCCESSOR

The vice president's most important duty—or, as some would argue, its sole reason for existence—is to succeed the president in the case of death, resignation, or incapacitation.

In our nation's history, nine vice presidents have ascended to the White House following the death or resignation of a president. Four of the presidents died of natural causes, four were assassinated, and only one resigned.

Given the ambiguities in the Constitution regarding the specific nature of presidential succession (that is, whether the vice president assumed the presidency itself, or just the powers of the presidency), the first four vice presidents to take office through succession were considered by many to be illegitimate. This sentiment was so strong that all four—John Tyler, Millard Fillmore, Andrew Johnson, and Chester Arthur—failed to win renomination by their own parties for an independent term of their own. None of the four served with any distinction, and Andrew Johnson was actually impeached over a political decision.

Theodore Roosevelt was the first vice president elevated to office to win a full term on his own, when he trounced Democrat Alton Parker in 1904. Ironically, the Republican Party bosses had chosen Roosevelt as William McKinley's running mate because they disliked Roosevelt's progressive platform as governor of New York and wanted to put him in a position where he would be powerless!

When Harry S. Truman took office following Franklin Roosevelt's death in 1945, the United States was at war with Germany and Japan. Roosevelt had kept Truman in the dark about the development of the atomic bomb, so it came as a great surprise to Truman when he was informed of the weapon only hours after being sworn in as president.

Twenty-Fifth Amendment

Following President Kennedy's assassination in 1963, political leaders realized that it was time to clarify the succession process. In 1967 the Twenty-Fifth Amendment was ratified. It established four points:

1. In the case of the president's death or removal from office, the vice president becomes president.
2. If the office of vice president is vacated, the president must nominate a new vice president, to be confirmed by a majority in both houses of Congress.
3. If the president is temporarily unable to discharge the duties of the office, he must inform both the Speaker of the House and the president pro tempore of the Senate in writing, at which time the vice president becomes acting president. Once the president is able to resume his duties, he must again inform both Congressional leaders in writing.
4. If a majority of the cabinet members (as well as the vice president) determine that the president is unable to discharge the powers of the office, they must inform the Speaker of the House and the president pro tempore in the Senate in writing, at which time the vice president would become acting president.

SELECTING A VICE PRESIDENT

For most of the nineteenth century, the vice presidential candidate was selected by party bosses, and was usually the result of "backroom" negotiations and compromises among various factions of the party. The presidential candidates typically had little input into this decision.

It has now become routine that shortly after securing his party's nomination, the candidate forms a search committee composed of his closest advisers to produce a shortlist of potential running mates. This committee usually completes its work by early summer, and in most cases the presidential candidate chooses someone from that shortlist. The selection is usually unveiled prior to the party convention as a way to generate extra buzz and momentum.

Factors to Consider

Modern presidential candidates take into account a combination of factors when narrowing down the list of potential running mates:

- *Regional Balance.* Having separate regions of the country represented on the presidential ticket is a frequent consideration. In 1988, Massachusetts Governor Michael Dukakis selected Texas Senator Lloyd Bentsen as his running mate. Bentsen was well known and regarded in the South, while Dukakis's base of support was in the Northeast.
- *Ideological Balance.* Like regional balance, ideological balance also helps a presidential ticket appeal to a wider audience. In 1980, Ronald Reagan selected George H.W. Bush primarily because Bush's moderate views helped lessen concerns among some voters that Regan was too conservative.
- *Carrying a State.* In some instances, the need to carry an important state is the key factor in choosing a running mate. In 1952, Dwight Eisenhower chose to run with California Senator Richard Nixon, whom he did not like, because he liked California's electoral votes more than he disliked Nixon.
- *Buzz Factor.* Candidates far behind in the polls will sometimes select a running mate who can possibly change the dynamics of the election—in other words, introduce the "buzz factor." In 2008, John McCain chose Alaska Governor Sarah Palin as his running mate, hoping to both appeal to the Republican base and get the votes of women.

THE VICE PRESIDENT'S CAMPAIGN ROLE

Historically, vice presidential candidates have played a minor campaign role in presidential elections. It is widely believed that Americans cast their vote for the person leading the ticket and not the running mate. In 1988, the Democrats tried to make Senator Dan Quayle's relative youth and inexperience a campaign issue against George H.W. Bush, but it failed to register with the voters.

Over the past several decades, vice presidential candidates have begun to assume a larger role in the election. Increasingly, they have been called upon to serve as the campaign "hatchet man," cutting down the opposition with sharp attacks.

During a presidential campaign, the high point for the two presidential running mates is the vice presidential debate—this is the one time when the candidates for vice president get to square off. Notwithstanding the hype leading up to it, this debate usually takes a back seat to the presidential debates and rarely has an impact on the campaign. In 2000, Dick Cheney and Joe Lieberman showered each other with pleasantries and compliments during their only faceoff, in sharp contrast to the two candidates in the presidential debates.

On the Campaign Trail

The most memorable moment of the 1988 campaign came during the vice presidential debate, when Senator Dan Quayle compared his experience to that of John F. Kennedy, to which his opponent, Lloyd Bentsen, responded: "Senator, I served with Jack Kennedy. I knew Jack Kennedy. Jack Kennedy was a friend of mine. Senator, you're no Jack Kennedy." It is one of the most often repeated lines in politics.

THE CABINET

The President's Circle of Advisers

A nonelected cabinet advises the president. This idea of the cabinet's role has its roots in the British system of government. In the seventeenth century, the English Parliament devised the "cabinet council"—a small group of men who advised the king on political issues and administered certain government departments—as a way to curb abuses by the monarch.

CABINET AND THE ARTICLES OF CONFEDERATION

The British idea was borrowed by the U.S. Congress under the Articles of Confederation. Just months after the ratification of the Articles of Confederation, the Congress set up the Department of Foreign Affairs and appointed Robert Livingston as the Secretary of Foreign Affairs— the first cabinet officer in our nation's history. Ten years later, the Department of Foreign Affairs was renamed the State Department.

IN THE CONSTITUTION

The role of the president and his advisers was one of the most hotly contested issues at the Constitutional Convention. A majority of the delegates agreed that a weak president was preferable to one that resembled a monarch, but disagreed over how best to restrict his authority.

Unable to reach a consensus, the framers decided on a single executive with limited powers, and purposely omitted any reference to a cabinet in the Constitution so as not to give credence to the notion of a "President by council."

Avoid a Feeble Executive

In Federalist No. 70 of *The Federalist Papers*, Alexander Hamilton—one of the few proponents of a strong executive—argued that it was undemocratic and unworkable to have a system in which a nonelected cabinet could overrule an elected president. "A feeble Executive implies a feeble execution of government," he concluded.

Among the many precedents established during Washington's presidency, the role of the cabinet ranks near the top of the list in importance. Washington believed that cabinet staff should serve as policy advisers and department managers. He frequently convened his cabinet as group meetings to discuss both specific departmental items and general matters of national governance. However, Washington never considered the cabinet an instrument for collective policymaking. Instead, he viewed it as a forum for open discussion and debate on national issues.

However, with the rise of political parties, and the advent of the patronage system, much of Washington's philosophy regarding cabinet appointments was lost on future generations. Cabinet selection, for the most part, simply became another opportunity for the president to reach out to various interest groups and strengthen his political base.

NAME THAT CABINET DEPARTMENT

As of 2016, there are fifteen cabinet departments.

1. *Department of Agriculture.* This department conducts research to improve agricultural activity, provides assistance to farmers and ranchers, and works to protect national forests from fire and disease.

2. *State Department.* Established in 1789, this department develops foreign policy, negotiates treaties, and handles diplomatic relationships with foreign governments. Its head is the first cabinet official to succeed to the presidency in the case of national disaster.

3. *Interior Department.* Established in 1849, its primary responsibility is to supervise Native American affairs. It also oversees the national parks system and is responsible for wildlife conservation.

4. *Department of Housing and Urban Development.* The mission of this department is to create affordable housing and home ownership opportunities for all Americans.

5. *Department of Labor.* This agency is responsible for setting workplace conditions, and monitoring contract negotiations between unions and management.

6. *Department of Defense.* By far the largest cabinet department with almost 700,000 employees, this agency provides for the national defense, manages the armed forces, and operates military facilities.

7. *Justice Department.* This department enforces federal criminal laws and provides legal advice to the president. It was formed

in 1789, although it did not become a cabinet-level department until 1870.

8. *Department of Veterans Affairs.* Created in 1988, this department promotes the welfare of veterans of the U.S. Armed Forces. It is estimated that more than 500,000 veterans and their spouses receive benefits from this agency every year.

9. *Commerce Department.* The purpose of this department is to promote economic growth and job creation, and protect the interest of businesses. It's also responsible for the national census, patents and trademarks, and promoting U.S. travel and tourism.

10. *Department of Homeland Security.* Established in 2002, this department's primary responsibility is to protect Americans at home from terrorist attacks. Airport luggage checkers, the Coast Guard, the border patrol, and many others now report to this agency.

11. *Department of Transportation.* This department is responsible for providing safe and easy travel within the United States. Its sub-agencies include the Federal Aviation Administration (FAA), the Federal Highway Administration (FHWA), and the National Transportation Safety Board (NTSB), which investigates plane crashes and other transportation-related accidents.

12. *Energy Department.* Established in 1977, this department is responsible for promoting the conservation of energy and resources, conducting research and development for alternative energy sources, and overseeing radioactive and nuclear materials at home and abroad.

13. *Department of Health and Human Services.* Originally created in 1953, this department promotes the health and welfare of the American people, and is the largest grant-making agency in the

federal government. The Food and Drug Administration (FDA) and Centers for Disease Control and Prevention (CDC) are just two of the many sub-agencies that report into this department.

14. *Department of Education.* The smallest cabinet department, with approximately 5,000 employees, this agency coordinates federal programs and policies meant to improve the quality of education nationwide.

15. *Treasury Department.* One of the three original cabinet departments established in 1789, it oversees the nation's fiscal policy and economy and is also responsible for protecting the president and his family.

No Guarantee to Last

Although the tendency in the past two centuries has been to create new cabinet departments, in some cases departments may be downgraded in status. For instance, the Department of Navy, formerly a cabinet department, eventually merged with other departments to form the Department of Defense. In theory, cabinet departments can be dissolved as well, although this has never occurred.

THOSE WHO SERVE IN THE CABINET

Putting together a cabinet is one of the first orders of business for a president-elect. Generally speaking, the composition of a president's cabinet reflects his political philosophy.

The head of the president's transition team usually chairs a search committee that puts together a shortlist of potential cabinet secretaries for each post. An extensive background check is done for the persons on the shortlist (with their permission), and the president typically interviews multiple candidates for each position.

Presidents take into account several factors when selecting their cabinet members:

- *Longtime friends.* Every president has included longtime friends—people he had known for decades—in his cabinet. Former Secretary of Labor Robert Reich first met President Clinton while in their early twenties when the two studied at Oxford University. President John F. Kennedy raised a few eyebrows when he appointed his brother Robert as attorney general.
- *Campaign loyalists.* It's not unusual for a president to fill a spot or two in his cabinet with campaign loyalists who had helped get him elected. Richard Daley, heir to the famed Daley political machine in Chicago, was rewarded for his campaign service with the top job at the Commerce Department during Bill Clinton's second term.
- *Member of the opposite party.* It has become a semi-tradition that at least one member of the opposite party be included in the cabinet. President Obama appointed Republican Ray LaHood secretary of transportation in his first cabinet.
- *Superstar.* Presidents often search out political "superstars" to serve in their cabinet for the expertise and prestige they bring to the administration. During the election of 2000, candidate George W. Bush let it be known that former chairman of the Joint Chiefs of Staff Colin Powell would be included in a Bush administration.
- *Elected officials.* Most cabinets include members and former members of Congress. Barack Obama nominated Kathleen

Sebelius for secretary of the Department of Health and Human Services.

- *Experts from the private sector.* Most presidents look to the private sector to fill one or two cabinet positions. For example, President Clinton chose longtime educator and University of Wisconsin-Madison President Donna Shalala to head the Department of Health and Human Services, where she served for eight years.

EXECUTIVE OFFICE OF THE PRESIDENT, POLICY "CZARS," AND NONGOVERNMENTAL ADVISERS

Helping the President

Throughout the nineteenth century and into the twentieth, the cabinet played a critical role in advising and counseling the president. During those years, outside of personal servants, clerical helpers, and aides, the president had almost no White House staff to help with the administration of the executive branch.

This all changed, however, with the dramatic expansion of the federal government during Franklin Roosevelt's administration. As the New Deal became law, dozens of agencies were created to administer the new programs. Roosevelt understood that the White House required increased staff to properly administer and oversee these new federal programs.

EXECUTIVE OFFICE OF THE PRESIDENT

In 1939, President Roosevelt proposed a major reorganization of the executive branch. Although Congress rejected most of FDR's proposal, it authorized the creation of the Executive Office of the President (EOP) as a way to staff the White House. In its first year, the EOP created six positions to help Roosevelt discharge his duties. Today, the EOP consists of ten staff agencies with more than 600 employees working at the White House.

Of the ten staff agencies created by the EOP, four in particular make up the majority of the White House staff:

1. *White House Office.* Established in 1939, it is the oldest and most influential staff agency within the White House. Personnel in this department include the chief of staff, press secretary, communications director, legal counsel, appointments secretary, senior advisers, and others who look out for the political interests of the president.

2. *National Security Council.* Created at the onset of the cold war, the primary function of the National Security Council (NSC) is to advise the president on domestic and foreign policy matters involving national security. The council consists of nineteen members, including the vice president, secretary of defense, secretary of state, and the national security adviser, one of the most high-profile positions in the administration.

3. *Council of Economic Advisers.* Established in 1946, this three-member group advises the president on issues relating to the economy. Its main responsibility is to devise economic policy and prepare the president's annual economic report to Congress.

4. *The Office of Management and Budget.* Reorganized during the Nixon administration, the primary responsibilities of the Office of Management and Budget (OMB) are to prepare the annual budget, help set fiscal policy, and supervise the administration of the federal budget.

The Staff's Roles

As the Executive Office of the President has grown in size, so too have its responsibilities. Because campaign loyalists, personal friends, and longtime allies of the president fill a vast majority of the EOP positions, modern presidents have grown increasingly comfortable with their staffs setting policy direction, drafting legislation, devising legislative strategy, and communicating the agenda—tasks once handled primarily by the cabinet. The White House staff is also aided by its close proximity and regular access to the president—two crucial ingredients when exercising power in the executive branch.

Policy initiatives that originate from the cabinet are usually reviewed and sometimes revised by the White House staff before meeting the president's approval. At times, this process has been the source of friction between the White House and the cabinet. Richard Nixon believed that his cabinet was captive of the bureaucracy, and regularly encouraged his staff to undermine them. President Lyndon Johnson and his staff spent considerable time figuring out ways to circumvent his department heads.

Strained Relations

Relations between President Carter's staff and cabinet grew so strained that a presidential retreat was held at the Catoctin Mountains so that the two camps could work out their differences. Apparently, little was accomplished—not long after, the president fired nearly half of his cabinet and appointed a new chief of staff.

NONGOVERNMENTAL ADVISERS

Every president has sought the advice of friends and allies outside of government at one time or another. Typically, these advisers serve as unbiased "sounding boards" for the president—ones that don't have a bureaucratic constituency or staff territories to protect. Most presidents turn to them infrequently, and only for counsel on specific matters for which they offer a special expertise.

Andrew Jackson was the first and perhaps only president to rely exclusively on counsel from a small circle of friends. This group was dubbed the "Kitchen Cabinet" by the press because they sneaked through the White House kitchen to meet with him. President Franklin Roosevelt had a similar group of informal advisers, whom he referred to as "the brain trust."

Hop and Franklin

President Roosevelt's closest informal adviser, Harry Hopkins, actually lived in the White House residence for long stretches of time during World War II. Roosevelt liked having "Harry the Hop" nearby, and believed it was better for the chronically ill Hopkins to be looked after by the White House staff. Hopkins and Roosevelt died within a year of each other.

President Obama maintained several such close advisers, particularly his longstanding friend Valerie Jarrett, who served as Senior Adviser to the President.

THE SUPREME COURT

Arbiter of Legislative Power

On the first Monday of each October, the U.S. Supreme Court begins a new session. Between October and July, it rules on eighty to 100 cases, and, in the process, creates and refines a body of case law. Some decisions will go unnoticed; others will please, anger, or activate Congress and the president, interest groups, the media, and the public. While the membership of the court is constantly in flux, its mission has remained the same: to interpret the meaning of the Constitution and determine the constitutionality of the laws that govern our land.

THROUGH THE CENTURIES

In the eighteenth century, the Supreme Court produced few important rulings. The justices spent a good deal of time on administrative functions as they tried to figure out the role of the court. It wasn't until the landmark decision of *Marbury v. Madison* in 1803, which established the principle of judicial review, that the court began to assert itself.

Nineteenth-Century Court

From 1801 through 1835, Chief Justice John Marshall—the longest-serving chief justice in history—guided the court through a period of rapid expansion in its power. Marshall was a strong believer in the preeminence of the federal government, and his views pervaded the court's decisions.

John Marshall's successor, Chief Justice Roger Taney, took a narrow interpretation of the Constitution. Under his tenure, the court found fewer federal powers and more states' rights than did the Marshall Court. Its philosophy led to the *Dred Scott* decision of 1857, considered by many to be the low point in Supreme Court jurisprudence. The *Scott* decision ruled that slaves were not citizens of the United States, and that laws prohibiting slavery violated the Constitution. *Scott* was later overturned by the Fourteenth Amendment.

Over the next seventy years, the Supreme Court continued to look suspiciously at the growth of the federal government. It crafted extremely narrow interpretations of the Civil Rights Amendments. In *Plessy v. Ferguson* (1896), the court concluded that the Fourteenth Amendment did not prohibit segregation, so long as it was "separate but equal." The doctrine survived until 1954, when the Supreme Court reversed itself in *Brown v. Board of Education*.

Twentieth-Century Court

During Franklin Roosevelt's presidency, the Supreme Court underwent another dramatic transformation. As justices hostile to the New Deal began retiring, Roosevelt replaced them with liberal jurists who believed that the federal government had broad power to regulate commerce and the economy.

Stare Decisis

In most of its cases, the Supreme Court operates on the legal principle known as stare decisis. According to this principle, precedent binds the current ruling. The practical upshot is that although membership in the court changes, justices are generally reluctant to overrule previous decisions. However, this has been done in some cases (as for example, in *Brown v. Board of Education*, which overruled *Plessy v. Ferguson*).

Over the next forty years, particularly during the tenure of Chief Justice Earl Warren (1953–1969), the Supreme Court aggressively pursued an agenda of expanded civil rights, civil liberties, and business regulation. *Brown v. Board of Education* ended school segregation; *Gideon v. Wainwright* created the right to counsel in criminal proceedings; *Miranda v. Arizona* established that police must inform suspected criminals of their rights (known as the Miranda Rights); and *Roe v. Wade* expanded the right to privacy to include the right to an abortion.

However, beginning with Chief Justice William Rehnquist in 1986, the court moved back toward a more narrow interpretation of the Constitution. The Rehnquist Court, and the court presided over by John Roberts as of 2005, eroded some of the criminal rights established by previous courts and chipped away at the right to privacy, including abortion.

APPOINTING JUSTICES

Filling a Supreme Court vacancy ranks among the most important decisions a president can make. Over the past two decades, the composition of the Supreme Court has become an increasingly prominent issue in the presidential election. This reached a height in early 2016 with the death of conservative Justice Antonin Scalia. Immediately following his death, the Republican senatorial leadership announced they would not consider any appointee proposed by President Barack Obama. Their clear hope was that the fall 2016 election would result in a Republican president, who could then appoint another conservative justice.

When choosing a nominee to the Supreme Court, presidents take into consideration several factors:

- *Ideology.* Over the past two decades, ideology has become the predominant consideration. President Clinton's appointments of Ruth Bader Ginsburg and Stephen Breyer, jurists generally considered moderate, reflected his centrist approach to governing. Not surprisingly, Ronald Reagan appointed Justice Antonin Scalia, considered by many to be among the most conservative members of the court in recent history. President Obama appointed Sonia Sotomayor and Elena Kagan, both generally liberal.
- *Confirmability.* Given the increased politicization of the confirmation process, the likelihood of the nominee being confirmed by the Senate is a factor that has grown in importance.
- *Age.* Because it's a lifetime appointment, age can be the deciding factor if two candidates are otherwise equally matched. In addition to being a reliably conservative vote, Clarence Thomas's relative youth—he was forty-three at the time of his nomination—made him an attractive appointment.
- *Race and gender.* It's undeniable that both race and gender play a role in today's nominating process. It was no coincidence that an African American, Clarence Thomas, replaced Thurgood Marshall, the court's first black justice. Sonia Sotomayor is the first Hispanic appointed to the court. Sandra Day O'Connor, appointed by President Reagan, was the court's first female justice.

MAKING IT TO THE SUPREME COURT

Not every legal action can be appealed to the highest court in the land—the Supreme Court must have jurisdiction in order to hear a case. This can be achieved one of two ways.

Original Jurisdiction

Article III, Section 2 of the Constitution gives the Supreme Court jurisdiction as the trial court over certain types of cases. These cases of original jurisdiction may be brought directly to the Supreme Court and are adjudicated (judged) only once without the possibility of appeal. The Constitution lists seven types of disputes that are entitled to original jurisdiction:

1. Cases arising under treaties
2. Cases affecting ambassadors
3. Cases of maritime jurisdiction
4. Cases between two states
5. Cases in which the U.S. government is a party
6. Cases between a state and a citizen of another state
7. Cases between states and foreign countries or citizens

Appellate Jurisdiction

Most disputes reach the Supreme Court through its appellate jurisdiction, meaning that the case has already been decided by either the lower federal courts or a state supreme court.

Cases arising through the federal court system begin in the U.S district courts, and involve disputes between citizens of two different states or criminal violations of federal law, such as the interstate trafficking of drugs, murdering a federal law enforcement official, espionage, and so on. The losing side can appeal the decision to one of thirteen U.S. courts of appeals, which are divided among geographic circuits. Whichever party loses in the court of appeals can make a final appeal to the Supreme Court. Most cases of appellate jurisdiction arise through the federal courts system.

Cases arising through the state courts system follow a similar route, only at the state level: A trial court makes a ruling, the losing party can appeal to the state court of appeals, and that loser can appeal to the state supreme court. All state remedies must be exhausted before the U.S. Supreme Court can consider hearing the case on appellate jurisdiction. With disputes arising through the state court system, an extra requirement is necessary to establish appellate jurisdiction: The appellant must show that an issue of federal law is in dispute. This may seem odd, since cases involving federal law are always settled in federal court, not state court. However, in some cases arising under state law, issues of federal law—such as the violation of a constitutional right (the right to free speech, right to due process, etc.)—are raised and must be resolved at the Supreme Court. In those situations, the Supreme Court can only rule on the federal issue in question. It cannot reexamine matters of state law involved in the case.

JUDICIAL REVIEW

Saying What the Constitution Means

In the strictest terms, judicial review is the authority of the courts to determine whether acts of Congress, the executive branch, and the states are constitutional. However, the concept is nowhere to be found in the Constitution; it was established by the Supreme Court in a landmark case called *Marbury v. Madison*, to this day considered the most important decision in Supreme Court history.

Exercising Judicial Review

Although the Supreme Court established the power of judicial review in 1803, it used it infrequently through the first part of the nineteenth century. In fact, prior to the Civil War only two federal laws were declared unconstitutional. On the other hand, during the 1930s the court aggressively used judicial review to strike down dozens of New Deal laws and regulations.

MARBURY V. MADISON

Shortly before leaving office in 1801, President John Adams appointed William Marbury the federal justice of the peace. The new president, Thomas Jefferson, then ordered his secretary of state, James Madison, to refuse to recognize Marbury's appointment. In response, Marbury filed a lawsuit against Madison, claiming that Madison's failure to recognize his appointment violated Section 13 of the Judiciary Act of 1789.

Supreme Court Chief Justice John Marshall despised Thomas Jefferson and believed that Marbury should be given his commission.

Marshall knew, however, that if he ruled in favor of Marbury, Jefferson would certainly ignore his decision, and the authority of the Supreme Court would be weakened. He also knew that if he ruled in favor of Jefferson, it would appear that he was bowing to political pressure, no doubt undermining the court's independence.

Faced with this dilemma, Marshall conjured a brilliant solution. He ruled against Marbury, stating that the Supreme Court could not hear the case because Section 13 of the Judiciary Act of 1789, which Marbury claimed granted the Supreme court authority to hear such cases, was itself unconstitutional. In doing this, Marshall established that the Supreme Court had the inherent power to declare acts of Congress unconstitutional, while at the same time not inviting retaliation from Thomas Jefferson, who was delighted that Marbury was denied his commission.

JUDICIAL REVIEW TODAY

Today, courts at both the national and state level have the power to determine the constitutionality of legislative acts. This aspect of American jurisprudence stands apart from most other Western democracies, in which only the highest courts (if any) exercise the power of judicial review.

The Supreme Court's decisions are seldom unanimous. Sometimes there is not even a full majority behind the written opinion "for the Court." There may, however, be additional justices who concur with that opinion but for different reasons. Regardless, the result is a majority decision that carries the day. Justices who disagree usually write a dissent, or a dissenting opinion.

THE FEDERAL AND STATE JUDICIARY

The Shape of the Courts

One of the many shortcomings of the Articles of Confederation was that it lacked a national judiciary. The delegates who gathered in Philadelphia for the Constitutional Convention in 1787 realized this, and set out to correct the problem.

However, there were great differences over the exact shape of the judicial branch. The Federalists, proponents of a strong national government, believed that the federal judiciary should consist of trial courts, appellate courts, and one supreme tribunal. The antifederalists, supporters of states' rights, were concerned that an integrated federal judiciary would usurp the states' authority and embolden the federal government.

The debate ended in compromise: "The judicial Power of the United States shall be vested in one supreme Court, and in such inferior Courts as the Congress may from time to time ordain and establish." Essentially, it was left to Congress to resolve the issue.

Congress wasted little time in doing just that, passing the Judiciary Act of 1789 in its very first session. The bill constructed a three-tier federal judiciary by adding a trial and appellate level. At the same time, it limited the jurisdiction of the federal courts, set a high monetary threshold for diversity cases (cases where the litigants are from different states), and gave the state courts concurrent jurisdiction over many federal issues. In the end, both sides were satisfied with the outcome. The fact that federal judiciary has changed so little over the past two centuries is a testament to its genius.

FEDERAL AND STATE CONSTITUTIONS

The Constitution of the United States is the supreme law of the land—no law, regardless of its source, can contravene it. Any law found in violation of the Constitution can be declared unconstitutional by the Supreme Court. Over the course of 200 years, the Supreme Court has compiled a vast body of constitutional law based on its interpretation of various phrases and clauses found in the Constitution. These interpretations, of course, have sometimes varied from court to court, which is how the law evolves over time.

Likewise, state constitutions are the supreme law within their respective borders, unless they contradict the U.S. Constitution, an act of Congress, or the provisions of a foreign treaty. Just as the Supreme Court interprets the Constitution, so does the highest court in each of the states interpret its own state's constitution.

Legislative Acts

Every year, tens of thousands of legislative bodies promulgate new laws and regulations that govern our lives, covering everything from zoning rules to highway speeds, the disposal of hazardous waste, and criminal conduct. Congress and the state legislatures are the best known of these bodies, but county, municipal, and district governments also contribute to statutory law.

Case Law

Through the years, decisions rendered by the various courts have formed a body of law referred to as "case law." Unlike statutory law or administrative regulations, which are codified and highly organized, case law is found in court opinions, and is generally tied to the particular facts of a case. Sometimes case law is referred to as "unwritten law," although this is a misnomer.

Case law differs from statutory law in that it is flexible, and can evolve over time to reflect society's changed values. To some extent, it is the ability of case law to adapt to the times that has helped make the Constitution a "living document," as many scholars refer to it.

In theory, it's the role of Congress and the president (the two elected branches of government) to make public policy, and it's the job of the courts (the appointed branch) to interpret and apply the law. In reality, however, judges make policy all the time when carrying out this task. This is made possible by the doctrine of judicial review.

Roe v. Wade

The landmark abortion case *Roe v. Wade* highlights the differing judicial philosophies. Proponents of the decision believe that the Supreme Court properly found that the U.S. Constitution guarantees the right to an abortion as part of its right to privacy, while opponents contend that the court circumvented the will of elected officials by reading new rights into the Constitution.

Judicial Activism and Restraint

There are two primary schools of thought when it comes to exercising judicial review. "Activist" judges and justices generally believe that the courts should aggressively use judicial review to thwart acts of Congress, executive agencies, and the state legislatures when they find those acts to be excessive in authority or contrary to public policy. "Restraintist" judges and justices, on the other hand, believe that the courts should defer to the judgment of the elected branches of government on legislative matters, and they tend to withhold using judicial review except in cases where a law or rule is clearly unconstitutional.

Today, judicial activism is generally associated with political liberalism, while judicial restraint is linked to conservatism. Democratic presidents typically appoint activist judges and justices who view the courts as vehicles for social change and betterment; Republican presidents typically appoint restraintist judges and justices who believe the courts should have a limited role in making public policy.

THE FEDERAL COURT SYSTEM

Think of the federal judicial system as a pyramid: The Supreme Court is on top, followed by an appellate level just below, and the district (or trial) courts at the base. The power flows downward, so the inferior courts are bound by the Supreme Court's decisions. However, all courts may exercise the same power of judicial review.

District Courts

The U.S district courts represent the starting point into the federal judicial system. Created by Section 2 of the Judiciary Act of 1789, the 94 district courts—staffed by more than 600 judges—are the trial courts for the federal judiciary. Every state (plus the District of Columbia, Guam, Puerto Rico, the Virgin Islands, and the Northern Mariana Islands) has at least one district court, and the larger states have several (New York, California, and Texas are the only states with four district courts). Each district court has more than one judge presiding, which allows for multiple trials to take place simultaneously (the Southern District of New York, which consists of Manhattan and the Bronx, has the most with twenty-eight judges).

The district courts hear three types of cases. The most common are criminal matters, which are initiated by the U.S. attorney for that district. Federal income tax evasion, counterfeiting U.S. currency, and trafficking narcotics across state lines are examples of criminal cases that would be tried at the district court. It also tries civil cases when the dispute is based on matters of civil law, such as contractual obligations, copyright infringement, unlawful trademark infringement, and the like. The least common are public law cases, in which citizens or private organizations sue governmental agencies for failing to act in accordance with their statutory obligations.

Court of Appeals

Losers at the district court can appeal to the U.S. court of appeals. The appellate courts are divided among thirteen geographic circuits, and they hear appeals from the district courts located within their respective circuits. The circuits are divided as follows:

1. Maine, New Hampshire, Rhode Island, Massachusetts, Puerto Rico
2. New York, Connecticut, Vermont
3. Pennsylvania, New Jersey, Delaware
4. West Virginia, Maryland, Virginia, North Carolina, South Carolina
5. Texas, Mississippi, Louisiana
6. Michigan, Ohio, Kentucky, Tennessee
7. Wisconsin, Illinois, Indiana

8. North Dakota, South Dakota, Minnesota, Nebraska, Iowa, Missouri, Arkansas
9. California, Nevada, Arizona, Oregon, Washington, Idaho, Montana, Hawaii, Alaska, Guam, Northern Mariana Islands
10. Utah, Wyoming, Colorado, Kansas, Oklahoma, New Mexico
11. Alabama, Georgia, Florida
12. District of Columbia
13. The Federal Circuit (no geographic jurisdiction)

The appellate courts have no discretion to refuse cases—they must accept all appeals brought before them. Because they are not trial courts, the appellate courts only review questions of law (whether the law was properly applied to the facts), not questions of fact (such as whether an event really took place). Because the Supreme Court takes very few cases, court of appeals rulings are rarely overturned.

GETTING INTO FEDERAL COURT

There is no automatic right to appear in federal court. In fact, the overwhelming majority of legal actions that occur in the United States take place in state courts, not the federal court. Two requirements must be met before an action can be judged in the federal system: jurisdiction and standing.

Jurisdiction

The federal judiciary is composed of courts of limited jurisdiction, meaning it can only hear cases where there is express authority to do so. Article III, Section 2 of the U.S. Constitution dictates two such situations. The first is when the disputed matter involves a question of federal law. The "federal question" can derive from the Constitution, an act of Congress, an executive branch ruling, or a dispute arising under a treaty.

The second type of federal jurisdiction occurs when the litigating parties are citizens of different states. This is "diversity of citizenship" jurisdiction. The amount in controversy must exceed $75,000, however, in order for diversity jurisdiction to be established. Disputes between U.S. citizens and foreign governments or citizens also satisfies diversity requirements.

Standing

In order to bring suit in federal court, the moving party (the party bringing the lawsuit) must have legal "standing." Standing is simply another way of saying that the litigant is entitled to appear before the court. Four conditions must be present to show standing:

1. There must be a conflict. Federal courts do not rule on hypothetical situations or give advisory opinions.
2. The plaintiff—or person bringing the action—must have been harmed in some way by the defendant, and there must be a remedy under the law for that harm.
3. The conflict at issue cannot be "moot," or have been resolved prior to adjudication.
4. There must be a specific plea alleged in the complaint. In order for a court to hear an action, the dispute must be based on a specific violation of law, whether it's a constitutional, statutory, or common law.

STATE COURTS

State courts serve the same function as the federal courts, except they function at the state level. They interpret the meaning of the state constitution, rule on matters of state statutory law, and create a body of state case law. Cases tried in state courts may deal with any of the following matters:

- Felony and misdemeanor crimes
- Business and real-estate disputes
- Divorce and child custody cases
- Will, estate, and trust probates
- Personal injury and other private tort actions
- Private economic (contract) disputes
- Matters involving state regulation of business and professional services

While no two state court systems are organized exactly alike, most states divide their court system among four general categories: trial courts of limited jurisdiction, trial courts of general jurisdiction, appellate courts, and the court of last resort.

Trial Courts of Limited Jurisdiction

Upward of 80 percent of all the courts in the United States are state courts of limited jurisdiction. These include juvenile courts, city courts, county courts, family courts, municipal courts, and magistrate courts. Typically, these courts hear minor cases, such as criminal misdemeanors (cases for which jail sentences would be less than one year), and civil disputes involving less than $1,000. These cases rarely go to trial—most are quickly resolved out of court.

Trial Courts of General Jurisdiction

Most states refer to their general jurisdiction courts as either district or superior courts. These courts handle major cases, such as felony crimes (cases for which jail sentences would be longer than one year), and civil disputes greater than $1,000. Most states divide their general trial courts into judicial circuits or regions according to existing boundaries, such as counties or parishes.

Intermediate Appellate Courts

As its name implies, appellate courts hear cases on appeal from the trial courts of limited and general jurisdiction. Only three-quarters of the states have intermediate appellate courts; the others designate their court of last resort as the sole court of appeal. In most situations, these appellate courts have mandatory jurisdiction, meaning that they must accept all cases brought before it.

Court of Last Resort

Every state has a highest court, or court of last resort. Most states refer to it as the supreme court, with New York being the notable exception (it calls it the court of appeals). For the most part, state courts of last resort behave similarly to the United States Supreme Court in that they have discretionary jurisdiction (they choose their cases), only rule on matters of law (they don't hear evidence), and are the final arbiters on matters of state law.

FEDERAL AND STATE COURTS

Defining the Powers of Government

There are vast areas of the law that the federal government does not deal with, everything from regulating the shores of inland lakes to sweeping the streets to determining the nature of marriage and the age of consent. Under the Tenth Amendment these powers are reserved to the states, and when a case involves them—such as a divorce, or a crime, such as burglary, that takes place totally within a single state—these cases must be brought in state courts.

Each state's courts are run according to that state's laws, subject only to the rights guaranteed to people by the Constitution and its amendments. Each state's courts have their own appeals route. You can get into the federal court system with a state court matter, but it needs to have "exhausted all state remedies"—that is, have appealed as far as possible within the state court system—or it needs to pose a federal question.

HOW THE FEDERAL COURTS ARE ORGANIZED

Under the Constitution, only one court is mandated: the Supreme Court. But Congress is empowered to create "inferior courts" as it deems necessary. Congress has been creating inferior courts since the Judiciary Act of 1789. Currently, these courts consist of district courts and circuit courts of appeals, as well as the U.S. Court of Federal Claims and the U.S. Court of International Trade.

There are also tribunals created by Congress as part of other agencies (including, sometimes, the courts). They include military courts martial, administrative judges who determine things like eligibility for disability payments under Social Security, and even federal magistrate courts (which take minor administrative hearings off the desks of district court judges) and bankruptcy courts. The judges in these courts do not serve for life but for limited terms; in addition, their salaries can be reduced. Magistrate judges and bankruptcy judges are appointed by the judges on the court of appeals under which they serve, and they have limited jurisdiction.

Limitations of Magistrate and Bankruptcy Courts

Court decisions have ruled that judges in these courts can't deprive anyone of life, liberty, or property but must stick to minor administrative matters. What this means is that their decisions can be appealed to the district court under which they serve, although a court trial is usually a much less efficient process than is an administrative hearing, and reversal is generally unlikely given the time and expense of a trial.

District Courts

There are ninety-four federal district courts. Every state has at least one judicial district; there is also one for the District of Columbia and one for the Commonwealth of Puerto Rico. In addition, there is a special U.S. Court of Federal Claims that hears claims against the U.S. government.

More populous states may have several districts, usually designated by their territory. The term "district court" refers to the class of court; each district court may have more than one judge. Each judge has a courtroom and staff; cases are assigned to different district judges on a random basis.

Although one of the judges in a district may be designated "chief judge" for administrative purposes, the judges have coequal power and occasionally make decisions that conflict as to principles of law. An appeal to the circuit court of appeals in which the district court sits may result in a ruling that will bind all district courts for that district, but not those of other circuits.

Circuit Courts

There are a dozen circuit courts of appeals, so named because originally, justices of the Supreme Court "rode the circuit" to hear appeals from various district courts. There may be a number of judges on any circuit court of appeals, but they usually appear in panels of three judges, although on some cases all of the judges for that circuit hear the trial together. This may happen in order to resolve the inconsistencies when different courts in the same circuit have issued conflicting rulings.

Courts in different circuits have coequal power and do not have to follow the decisions of courts in other circuits, although they may choose to do so. Often, cases are appealed to the Supreme Court to resolve differences between the rule in one circuit and that of another. Decisions made by a circuit court of appeals bind only the district courts in that circuit, not in other circuits.

There is also a U.S. Court of Appeals for the Federal Circuit. This court hears appeals from all district courts in patent matters and also hears appeals from the U.S. Court of Federal Claims.

Magistrates

Federal magistrate judges assist district court judges by hearing motions or holding preliminary hearings and scheduling hearings, so as to free up the district courts for trials. The magistrates may also hear prisoner appeals, like habeas corpus hearings.

Bankruptcy Courts

Bankruptcy judges are appointed by the circuit court of appeals in whose territory they serve. Cases are "referred" to them by the district court under which they serve, and their decisions are considered decisions of that court, but may be appealed to that court—or, if there is a bankruptcy appellate panel in that circuit, they may be appealed to that panel. Only five of the circuits have such panels. These panels are made up of bankruptcy judges from their circuit, and the judges serve in groups of three. Bankruptcy judges are appointed for fourteen-year terms.

THE FEDERAL APPEALS PROCESS

The normal route to an appeal in the federal courts is up the chain of command, but litigants do not have to wait until a trial is finished before appealing. Often, there will be an appeal from a decision on a motion. A "motion" is a legal petition to the court to do something that will affect a trial, such as compel testimony of a witness, or freeze assets pending the resolution of a trial. Litigants can also move to disallow certain evidence, that is, to keep it from presentation at trial. After the appellate court makes a ruling on this procedural matter, the trial resumes.

It is also possible to appeal a matter from a state court to the Supreme Court. The first time that occurred was in *Fletcher v. Peck*, in 1810. The current rule is that litigants must exhaust state remedies before appealing to the Supreme Court of the United States. This usually means litigants have appealed to, or been denied an appeal by, the highest court in their state.

There are occasions when a matter may be removed to a federal district court. This could occur, for example, when a matter brought in a state court turns out to be something preempted by federal law. This involves matters such as copyright disputes, bankruptcy hearings, or a federal habeas corpus hearing. On rare occasions, there may be a direct appeal to the Supreme Court that bypasses the court of appeals. This might happen when a law affecting the entire country, such as the military draft, is ruled unconstitutional by a district court. The Supreme Court is not obligated to accept the case, and may issue a decision saying that it is not "ripe." But if the case really is of national import, the Supreme Court may take it so as to issue a decision sooner.

When a Court Must Defer to Another Court

Rulings of the Supreme Court must be followed by all lower courts. On rare occasion, the opinion states that the matter is unique and need not be followed. For example, the controversial ruling of *Gore v. Bush*, which ultimately decided the presidential election of 2000, applied to only that case. Generally, courts are not bound by the decisions of other courts at their level, although they may take notice of a decision and incorporate it into their decision-making process. In other instances, they may take notice of it to specifically disagree with it.

When the superior court agrees with the lower court's ruling, it will usually *affirm*; when it disagrees, it will *reverse*. If it wants further information than the trial court provided, it may reverse and *remand*. A remand amounts to an order for the lower court to redecide the case in a manner that is consistent with the ruling of the higher court. Sometimes it will issue a hybrid ruling, reversing in part and affirming in part.

SEPARATION OF POWERS

Balancing State and Federal Governments

One of the most important powers of the federal government is to regulate commerce with foreign countries and among the states. Historically, Congress has broadly interpreted this power, and the courts have backed that up. Congress has used this grant of power to create interstate roads (even the portion of those roads that lies within a single state), to establish trademarks for businesses that deal in interstate matters, and to regulate the interstate shipment of food. And it uses the commerce power to create and enforce consumer protection laws, workplace protection laws, airline safety rules, and environmental protection laws.

The federal government has the power to create and regulate the country's money and punish counterfeiters; it can borrow money and levy taxes to pay for the cost of government. It also can declare war and maintain the military forces of the United States. The states too can maintain militias, but the president is commander in chief of the state militias as well as the U.S. military forces. Anything that concerns the country *as a whole* generally falls under the purview of the federal government.

POWERS OF THE STATES

So what powers are reserved to the states? Basically, the states hold every power that the federal government hasn't claimed for itself. However, a state cannot infringe on the rights of its people. So a state government cannot—at least since the passage of the Fourteenth

Amendment—curtail an individual's right to practice his or her religion (unless that religion includes harming someone else, like making human sacrifices). But it can govern the hours that restaurant owners can keep their businesses open.

Federal and State Crimes

Some crimes are a matter of federal law, such as committing mail fraud or counterfeiting. These cases are prosecuted in federal court because only the federal government has the right to regulate money and punish people who print their own. A U.S. district attorney appointed by the president (and confirmed by the Senate) prosecutes these cases in the local federal district court where the crime was committed.

Some crimes are a matter of state or local law, such as opening a restaurant without a license, driving the wrong way on a one-way street, snatching a purse, or committing murder. These offenses will be prosecuted by local district attorneys or even town or village attorneys, and will be brought into state or local courts.

Federal Murder and State Murder

Although murder generally falls within jurisdiction of state laws, if the victim is a federal official, or if the crime is committed on federal land (like a national park), it may constitute a federal crime.

Some crimes have concurrent jurisdiction, which means that they can be prosecuted in either the federal or state courts. Sometimes different elements of the same crime can be prosecuted in both kinds of courts. For example, beating up a person who is a member of a minority may be the crime of "battery" under state and local laws. But if the perpetrator choses the victim because of race or religion, the federal government might be able to prosecute for depriving the victim of his or her civil rights, which would be a federal crime.

Many crimes may also have a *civil* aspect. If a person beats up someone, the state may prosecute the perpetrator for the crime, but the victim may also sue for civil damages—hospital bill and lost wages, plus the pain and suffering as a result of the beating. If the crime has a federal aspect—if, for example, a person or entity infringed a copyright—that suit would be brought into a federal court rather than a state one. And sometimes the victim has a choice; if an individual runs over a person from another state, and causes the victim more than $75,000 in damages, the victim may have the choice of bringing suit in state court (where the accident happened) or in federal court under "diversity jurisdiction," which covers suits between citizens of different states that meet the minimum dollar amount set by federal law.

When Federal Law Trumps Local Laws

When the rights guaranteed to all persons in the United States are violated by state laws or local ordinances, or by state or local enforcement officials, individuals have both state and federal recourse. For example, individuals (or their attorneys) can move to dismiss a case brought in state court if the arrest was the result of an unreasonable search and seizure (something the Constitution protects everyone from). But if it is not dismissed, individuals can appeal the matter to federal court or even bring a separate federal lawsuit against those who they believe may have violated their civil rights.

IMMIGRATION MATTERS

There are two places in the Constitution that deal specifically with immigration matters. Section 8 of Article I gives Congress the power "To establish an uniform Rule of Naturalization." Under this power, Congress can decide who can become a naturalized American citizen, and under what circumstances. Congress has the power to create all laws "necessary and proper" to maintain its other powers and the powers granted to the government by the Constitution. As a result, Congress can and does make immigration policy.

CASE LAW EXPANDS THE MEANING OF THE CONSTITUTION

The United States comes from a common-law tradition. As such, it is a country where the written opinions of judges expand and explain the meaning of the Constitution and of the laws made pursuant to it. The requirement that there be a particular "case or controversy" to get into court means that the opinion of the court deals with a law's application under a specific fact situation: One person did something to another person, and the result was a circumstance that needs to be addressed. Case law could be interpreted as not unlike parables in the Bible: They explain how a rule works under specific circumstances.

Conflicts Between the States and a Strong Central Government

While not proclaiming the rights of the states quite as vociferously as does the Articles of Confederation, the Constitution supports both those states' rights and those of a strong central government. However, the more power the federal government claims for itself, the less the states will have. This creates a tension. In the mid-nineteenth century this tension nearly snapped the country in two by way of the Civil War.

Certainly the basic cause of the Civil War was slavery, but much of the conflict had to do with the rights of the states as opposed to those of the federal government. The Constitution fosters that conflict by guaranteeing certain powers to the states, just as it guarantees certain other powers to the central government.

The federal government is charged with, among other things, regulating commerce and conflicts among the states, maintaining an army and a navy, coining money, establishing weights and measures. In other words, it has all of the powers that are given to Congress, to the president, and to the Supreme Court. In some cases, when a power of the central government is stated in one part of the Constitution, this power is denied the states in another section, as though to emphasize where the powers actually reside. For example, in Article I, Congress is given the power to declare war; in Article II, the president is given the power to make treaties (with the advice and consent of the Senate). In case any of the states missed that, Section 10 of Article I reminds them that "No State shall enter into any Treaty, Alliance, or Confederation."

Section 10 re-lists many of the things Congress can do, and specifically forbids the states from doing them:

No State shall enter into any Treaty, Alliance, or Confederation; grant Letters of Marque and Reprisal; coin Money; emit Bills of Credit; make any Thing but gold and silver Coin a Tender in Payment of Debts; pass any Bill of Attainder, ex post facto Law, or

Law impairing the Obligation of Contracts, or grant any Title of Nobility.

No State shall, without the Consent of the Congress, lay any Imposts or Duties on Imports or Exports, except what may be absolutely necessary for executing it's inspection Laws: and the net Produce of all Duties and Imposts, laid by any State on Imports or Exports, shall be for the Use of the Treasury of the United States; and all such Laws shall be subject to the Revision and Controul of the Congress.

No State shall, without the Consent of Congress, lay any Duty of Tonnage, keep Troops, or Ships of War in time of Peace, enter into any Agreement or Compact with another State, or with a foreign Power, or engage in War, unless actually invaded, or in such imminent Danger as will not admit of delay.

Rights That Cannot Be Denied to the States

Similarly, certain rights are guaranteed to the states, both by the text of the Constitution (which guarantees them, among other things, a "Republican Form of Government") and by the Tenth Amendment, which notes that, "The powers not delegated to the United States by the Constitution, nor prohibited by it to the States, are reserved to the States respectively, or to the people."

Rights That Belong to the People

A republican form of government, which the Constitution guarantees to each of the states, still needs to keep order while it provides people with basic rights. The Constitution provides for states to maintain militias, for the federal government to call out those militias, and whatever else it needs to do to maintain order. It also states, in the Bill of Rights, that people have a right to free speech, a free press, freedom of religion, and the right to assemble and petition their government. But where does freedom to assemble begin and keeping the peace end?

Some of the conflicts that have developed in this modern era have dealt with the fine line where the rights of the people intersect with the need of the government to maintain order. Nowhere is this more obvious than with the implementation of the Patriot Act and dealings with enemy combatants after the attacks of September 11, 2001.

The WikiLeaks circumstances are a further example. (WikiLeaks, an organization dedicated to acquiring and releasing secret information, released a large number of State Department cables in 2010, potentially putting the lives of U.S. personnel around the globe in danger.)

The Constitution defines treason narrowly because English kings historically used that charge broadly, in order to get rid of their enemies. To commit treason, one must levy war against the United States, or "adhere" to the country's enemies, "giving them aid and comfort." Did the WikiLeaks publication of government documents constitute adhering to America's enemies? Or was it an exercise in generic freedom of expression?

Fair Trial and Free Press

The fact that the First Amendment of the Constitution guarantees freedom of the press has long created a situation that is problematic not only for those parts of the government that need to operate in secret for public safety purposes, like diplomacy and defense, but also the prosecution of criminals. This has only been aggravated since the advent of the Internet. Traditional newspapers and magazines employed professional journalists who usually veri-fied their stories, as well as editors who called upon them to provide a factual basis for what they published. But with a free and open Internet, anyone with a blog can post anything, whether it has been verified or not. Half-truths and outright lies can go viral, as can facts that would not be admissible in court.

Anonymous Internet posts can negate the right of an accused to face the person who has brought the accusations. Publication of unverified facts can contaminate the jury pool so that it is impossible for an accused to get a trial by an unbiased jury.

THE THREE BRANCHES STRUGGLE WITH EACH OTHER

The system of checks and balances that keeps one branch of the government from dominating the other two forces them all to work together to accomplish anything. But the independence of each branch makes them more likely to do battle with each other than to cooperate. This builds gridlock into the system, and the party system only compounds it. A government that stymies itself will have dif-ficulty oppressing its citizenry, and the framers were certainly aware of that.

The Bicameral Chamber Pits One House Against the Other

Having two distinct legislative chambers—a deliberative one with equal representation (Senate) and a population-based, more constituency-oriented one (House)—creates conflict in legislative function. Moreover, the staggered six-year terms of the Senate make a swift political turnover of that chamber less likely. This timing contributes to the odds that a party may predominate in one of the houses while another party predominates in the other. A partisan effort to counter the votes of the other chamber is built into the Constitution. In other words, the creation of gridlock was intentional.

The People versus the State

From the beginning of the republic, there has been a tension between the people and the government that ostensibly represents them. Inequitable representation is built into the way Congress is designed. The notion that every state, regardless of size or wealth, is allotted two seats in the Senate, and every state, no matter how small its population, is allotted at least one representative in the House, is itself contradictory to the idea of "one-man-one-vote." Even the House (although it ostensibly represents the people on a population basis), can never represent all of the people equally, when allocations of representation are by population divisions within states, as opposed to a portion of the population as a whole.

Civilian Checks on Military Power

The fact that the president, a civilian, is commander in chief of the armed forces keeps the military from asserting its power to stage a coup. The fact that Congress controls the appropriations, and must renew them every two years, also keeps the military in check. So does the fact that Congress is responsible for the rules that govern the armed forces.

THE CIVIL SERVICE

Turning the Wheels of Government

Although it's nowhere to be found in the Constitution, the federal bureaucracy is sometimes referred to as the fourth branch of government. Every chief executive has tried to bring the bureaucracy under his control, but few have succeeded. President Truman may have summed it up best as he was preparing to hand the reigns of government to President Eisenhower. "He'll sit here and he'll say, 'Do this! Do that!' *And nothing will happen*," Truman predicted. "Poor Ike—it won't be a bit like the Army."

BASIC ORGANIZATION

The federal bureaucracy is divided among four types of structures. In addition to cabinet departments, there are also three types of "noncabinet" agencies—independent executive agencies, independent regulatory commissions, and government corporations.

Independent Executive Agencies

Executive agencies are independent bureaucracies that are located outside the cabinet department structure. These agencies report directly to the president, who appoints and removes their chief officials. Presidents prefer an executive agency to remain independent when it has a narrow mission that requires special consideration.

There are approximately seventy independent executive agencies of varying sizes. Some employ tens of thousands of people; others, several hundred. The Central Intelligence Agency (CIA), Small Business Administration (SBA), National Aeronautics and Space Administration (NASA), Environmental Protection Agency (EPA), and the Peace Corps are independent executive agencies.

Independent Regulatory Commissions

These commissions are formed with the express purpose of regulating particular sectors of the economy and promulgating rules. They are intended to be totally independent from the president and the executive branch. Congress came up with independent regulatory commissions in order to delegate its oversight responsibilities without giving too much power to the executive branch.

Most regulatory commissions are run by boards of commissioners, who are appointed to fixed terms by the president and confirmed by the Senate. The appointments are bipartisan (no party can have more than a one-person majority), and the president cannot remove a commissioner absent any malfeasance. Most commissioners are either industry experts, academics, or former elected officials.

Government Corporations

Sometimes referred to as quasi-governmental agencies, these entities are created when the government activity is commercial in nature. Government corporations behave like private companies in that they generate revenues through buying and selling property, lending money, or participating in other market activities.

Like a private corporation, a government corporation is headed by a chief executive officer, who is chosen and supervised by a board of directors or commissioners. The board of directors is selected by the president, much the same way as for an independent regulatory commission. Unlike private corporations, however, a government corporation has no public shareholders, retains all its profits, and does not pay taxes. The United States Postal Service is the most recognizable government corporation. With almost 900,000 employees, it is the largest employer in the United States. The Federal Deposit Insurance Corporation (FDIC), Export-Import Bank, and Amtrak are also government corporations.

Government Sponsored Entities

Government corporations should not be confused with government-sponsored enterprises (GSEs), which are shareholder-owned companies that are chartered by the federal government to promote certain social policies, such as home ownership. The Federal National Mortgage Association (Fannie Mae), the Federal Home Loan Mortgage Corporation (Freddie Mac), and the Student Loan Marketing Association (Sallie Mae) are all GSEs.

THE BUREAUCRACY'S ROLE IN GOVERNMENT

The primary purpose of the bureaucracy is to administer the laws and policies passed by Congress and the president by establishing programs, promulgating rules and regulations, and creating infrastructures to deliver benefits in accordance with the language and intent of the enabling legislation. Sometimes, however, bureaucracies make policy as well. This occurs in two ways.

Iron Triangles

The term "iron triangle" is used to describe the alliance formed by Congress, bureaucrats, and interest groups to make public policy in the group's domain. These iron triangles are often referred to as "subgovernments," and typically operate outside the conscious view of Congress, the president, and the public.

Iron triangles have been making policy for several decades, and they operate on the theory of mutual self-interest. Bureaucrats are dependent on Congress for continued authorization and funding, so it is in their interest to work closely with Congressional committees and subcommittees that have jurisdiction over their departments. Likewise, members of Congress gladly solicit legislative input and direction from the interest groups in return for campaign contributions and electoral support. In the end, all parties benefit from the relationship: Congress receives campaign contributions, interest groups get favorable legislation, and bureaucrats preserve their jobs and enhance their standing.

Issue Networks

As the federal government has grown in size and complexity, policymaking has become more nuanced and subtle. With control of both houses of Congress and the White House changing more frequently than in previous eras, "issue networks" have begun to replace iron triangles as the preferred method of policymaking.

Issue networks are composed of individuals and groups that coalesce around a particular policy initiative and then lobby Congress, the president, the courts, and even the bureaucracy to adopt this public policy. Members of the issue network may include legislators, bureaucrats, scholars, activists, and even members of the media. It's not unusual for issue networks to form around opposing sides of the same policy debate.

WHO ARE THE BUREAUCRATS?

More than 90 percent of the federal workforce is composed of career civil servants—nonpolitical appointees who retain their positions regardless of the administration in the White House. Many of these career bureaucrats develop vast expertise and institutional knowledge regarding their particular niche and, in some cases, their own personal agendas.

In addition to career civil servants, the bureaucracy is also staffed by political appointees. For the most part, the president makes the appointments for top positions in the federal bureaucracy; rarely does Congress make any appointments.

It has been argued that, over time, some bureaucrats become more preoccupied with protecting their jobs than solving the problems of government. Through the years, countless elected and appointed officials have expressed frustration with having a class of career bureaucrats administering the agencies of government. To their thinking, it has contributed to institutional inertia and an increasingly unresponsive federal bureaucracy.

GETTING APPOINTED

How does one get appointed to a federal position? After every presidential election, the Government Publishing Office (GPO) publishes *United States Government Policy and Supporting Positions* (also known as "the plum book" because of all the plum positions listed). Beginning with the transition period and lasting well into the president's first year of office, the White House fills the positions listed in the "plum book."

The president takes into consideration a combination of factors—political affiliation, area of expertise, work experience, personal characteristics, and background—when selecting a candidate for a particular job. Thousands of appointments are made every year, most of which require Congressional approval. With the increased partisanship in Washington, it's not unusual for these positions to remain empty for months or even years at a time.

Most political appointees remain in their positions for a brief period of time; the average term is less than two years. This being the case, career civil servants are typically disinclined to aggressively implement their current boss's directives because it's likely that the appointed boss will be gone in a year or two.

PULLING THE PURSE STRINGS

Congress's most effective tool for controlling the bureaucracy is the authorization and appropriations process. When an agency is established, Congress must authorize funds for it. In some cases, such as the Social Security Administration (SSA), this is a permanent authorization, meaning it never has to be renewed. For others, such as NASA, this authorization is periodic—it must be renewed every few years.

Congress also controls the annual budgets for both permanently and periodically authorized agencies through the appropriations process. This gives Congress the ability to abolish or modify agency programs by eliminating or cutting back funding. Many times, Congress will make agency appropriations contingent upon specific policy changes. In rare cases, Congress will do just the opposite, giving increased funding beyond what was requested for programs it finds particularly effective. Agency heads periodically testify before the Congressional committees and subcommittees with jurisdiction to request increased funding.

Nonappropriations Methods

Congress also has several nonappropriations tools that it uses to oversee the bureaucracy—some more effective than others:

- *Hearings and investigations.* Congress can investigate agencies and call bureaucrats to testify before committees and subcommittees to determine whether the agency is complying with Congressional intent. It can also ask the Government Accountability Office (GAO) and the Congressional Budget Office (CBO) to investigate particular agency actions and conduct oversight studies.
- *Legislative vetoes.* The legislative veto allows Congress to reject (by majority vote) an agency's policy proposal or action.
- *Mandatory reports.* Congress can require agencies, departments, and even the president to periodically assess programs and report their findings. Through these reports, Congress can determine whether the laws it has passed are having their intended effect.

- *Inspectors General.* Virtually every agency has Inspectors General (IGs) that reside outside the bureaucratic chain of command. These inspectors regularly meet with Congress to report on waste, fraud, and abuse within the agency. On occasion, Congress will direct the IGs to perform specific audits and investigations on its behalf.

Bureaucratic Whistleblowers

The term "whistleblower" is used to describe someone who brings attention to (blows the whistle on) illegal or corrupt behavior, gross inefficiencies, or mismanagement. Whistleblowers show up in both the private and public sectors. Relying on whistleblowers for oversight is a recent phenomenon.

Bureaucratic whistleblowers play an important role in agency oversight. They have been an invaluable resource for Congress and the public for aiding understanding of bureaucratic waste, abuse, and corruption. Whistleblowers may be clerical workers, managers, experts, and even department leaders. Despite legislation that prohibits acts of retaliation against whistleblowers by their superiors, most government whistleblowers end up leaving their jobs within three years of coming forward with their information, for various reasons.

ATTEMPTS AT REFORM

As long as there has been a federal bureaucracy, there have been complaints about its inefficiency, ineffectiveness, arrogance, and lack of responsiveness to the public's needs. Poll after poll has revealed that government bureaucracies consistently rank among the most unpopular institutions in America.

Over the past several decades, Congress has made several attempts to reform the federal bureaucracy and rehabilitate its image. The Government in the Sunshine Act of 1976 requires that federal agencies run by a panel of executives hold their meetings in public sessions. The only exceptions to this rule are personnel matters and court proceedings. Every other type of agency gathering—whether formal or informal—is required to be open to the public, or "in the sunshine." This transparency has helped make some bureaucracies more responsive to Congress and the public.

Many states have adopted "sunset laws" as a way to gain greater control over their bureaucracies. Sunset laws create a finite lifespan for a bureaucracy and automatically terminate it at the end of that designated period, unless the bureaucracy is specifically reauthorized by the state legislature. In order to be reauthorized, these bureaucracies must prove their effectiveness and merit. It's only a matter of time before Congress makes greater use of sunset laws.

There has also been a growing trend at the state and federal levels to privatize certain government functions. Supporters of this approach contend that the private sector can provide some services more cost-effectively and with better results. Some prisons, schools, waste management facilities, and homeland security functions have been privatized in recent years. There is a limit, however, to the public services that private companies can perform.

SECURITY AGENCIES

Keeping Americans Safe

The United States has four key security agencies: the Federal Bureau of Investigation (FBI); the Central Intelligence Agency (CIA); the National Security Agency (NSA); and the Department of Homeland Security.

THE FBI

The Federal Bureau of Investigation (FBI) is the oldest of the security services. It was formed as the Bureau of Investigation (BOI) in 1908, in part because of fears of radicalized immigrants following the assassination of President William McKinley in 1901. The bureau was eventually moved under the authority of the Justice Department and renamed the Federal Bureau of Investigation.

In 1919–20, under the direction of a young man named J. Edgar Hoover, the FBI conducted a series of raids against foreign-born political activists, carried out at the instigation of Attorney General Mitchell Palmer. This marked a trend for the FBI that was to continue until Hoover's death in 1972—the FBI leadership saw the bureau as essential to America's fight against communist infiltration. During World War II, the bureau also played a leading role in rounding up and interning Japanese Americans.

Hoover compiled files not only on American activists but on leading political figures. This enabled him to remain in office long after many people felt he should have been removed. After his death, the

FBI became caught up in the Watergate scandal under the leadership of Hoover's successor, L. Patrick Gray. Since then the FBI has tried to rebuild its reputation, placing emphasis on integrity and efficiency.

Currently the FBI has more than 400 regional offices scattered throughout the United States. It also maintains some agents overseas, who coordinate with foreign intelligence services. The main headquarters of the agency is the J. Edgar Hoover Building in downtown Washington, D.C.

THE CIA

Rightly or wrongly, the Central Intelligence Agency (CIA) tends to get blamed for a lot of nefarious goings-on around the world. This is because it really has, on occasion, helped to overthrow governments and assassinate foreign politicians. Since the 1980s, the agency has been subject to a greater degree of oversight, which has helped curb its more egregious abuses.

The CIA grew out of American intelligence efforts during World War II, which were led by the Office of Strategic Services (OSS). The CIA was formally created in 1949. Although its charter directed it to gather intelligence, it proved inept; it failed completely to predict the entry of China into the Korean War, something that almost led to America losing the war. In 1953, the agency played a key role in overthrowing the Iranian government of Mohammad Mosaddegh. It would carry out a similar action in 1973 in Chile, sparking a military coup that overthrew the leftist government of Salvadore Allende.

The CIA has been implicated in numerous other coups or assassinations in:

- Syria (1949)
- Iran (1953)
- Guatemala (1954)
- Indonesia (1957)
- Dominican Republic (1960)
- Congo (1961)

The CIA was also heavily involved in attempts to assassinate Cuban leader Fidel Castro during the Kennedy administration. The agency has also been accused of domestic espionage, particularly during Richard Nixon's presidency.

The agency came under renewed scrutiny during the administration of George W. Bush, when it admitted that it maintained various "black sites" around the world where prisoners detained during the "War on Terror" were held and sometimes tortured. These practices stopped—or, at least, were said to have stopped—under the Obama administration.

THE NSA

The National Security Agency (NSA) is the most secretive of the security services. A joke says that the letters NSA stand for "No Such Agency." The NSA's role is to surreptitiously collect electronic information about other countries. Its charter specifically forbids it from eavesdropping on Americans.

Located at Fort Meade, Maryland, the NSA originated—like the CIA—during World War II, although the NSA was formally created only in 1952. It maintains powerful computer systems and has struggled in recent years with storage needs, given the volume of information it sweeps up.

Although the NSA is not supposed to spy on Americans, during the Vietnam War it intercepted communications by leaders of the antiwar movement in the United States if those communications were with people overseas. Since the outbreak of the war in Afghanistan and active American involvement in the Middle East, the NSA has been among the most important of the intelligence-gathering organizations. The Obama administration relied extensively on the NSA for data to track al-Qaeda, ISIS (Islamic State of Iraq and al-Sham), and other terrorist organizations.

Spying at Home

During the 1960s, the FBI maintained files on a large number of organizations that supported the Civil Rights Movement and opposed the war in Vietnam. Although the agency's worst abuses have been curbed, many are still suspicious that government surveillance of dissenting Americans has continued. In 2013 it was revealed that the NSA collected "metadata" on Americans through a program code-named PRISM. The issue of this collection of information has been hotly debated in regard to the balance of personal privacy rights versus the need for government to gather and analyze information about possible terror plots.

THE DHS

After the September 11, 2001, terror attacks in New York and Washington, the Bush administration decided to combine a number of security agencies under a single umbrella organization. Their intent was to improve communication and create a timely response to future emergencies. With more than 240,000 employees, the Department of Homeland Security (DHS) is the third-largest cabinet-level department (after Defense and Veterans Affairs). The DHS contains the following security agencies:

- U.S. Citizenship and Immigration Services
- U.S. Customs and Border Protection
- U.S. Immigration and Customs Enforcement
- U.S. Secret Service
- Transportation Security Administration
- U.S. Coast Guard
- Federal Emergency Management Agency

A host of smaller organizations also fall under the department. The formation of the department in 2002 was the biggest reorganization of the federal government since the creation of the Department of Defense.

One of the department's first actions was to create a color-coded "threat warning system" that would let the American people know about possible terrorist attacks. However, that system has been criticized as being both simplistic and alarmist.

How well the new department has functioned is difficult to calculate. Between 2001 and 2016, no major terrorist attacks occurred on U.S. soil. However, many have expressed concern at the size and bureaucratic inefficiency of the new department.

THE IMPORTANCE OF VOTING

Exercising the Right to Change the Government

Voting is a cornerstone of American democracy. It is among the most fundamental and important rights of every American. But the right to vote has not always been extended to all Americans.

THE RIGHT TO VOTE

The Founding Fathers created a government whereby the power to govern was established not by heredity but by the ballot box—a revolutionary idea. At first, the right to vote extended only to white Protestant males who owned property. As a result, only 6 percent of the population was eligible to vote in the first presidential election.

Throughout the nineteenth century, the right to vote was slowly extended to a wider segment of the population. Religious and property-owning restrictions were the first to be eliminated. By the middle of the nineteenth century, all white males were allowed to vote.

Women remain disenfranchised until the passage of the Nineteenth Amendment in 1920, which declared that voting could not be denied on the basis of gender. For African Americans, it was a longer and more difficult struggle to obtain full enfranchisement. Following the Civil War, the Fifteenth Amendment established that the federal and state governments could not discriminate against voters on the basis of race, color, or the previous condition of slavery. In theory, this should have given all African Americans the right to vote. In reality, however, it did little to bring African Americans into the electoral process, as Southern states used various tactics—literacy tests, poll taxes, and intimidation—to keep blacks away from the polls. As a consequence, well into the twentieth century only a small percentage of African Americans living in Southern states were able to vote. It wasn't until the Twenty-Fourth Amendment of 1964 and the historic Voting Rights Act of 1965 that all of these obstacles were removed. Today, every American citizen eighteen years of age or older is eligible to vote, though some states do not extend the vote to prisoners or felons.

DECLINING VOTER TURNOUT

Although the right to vote is one of our most precious rights, it has been exercised with declining frequency. At the presidential level, voter turnout has steadily declined over the past seventy years, as fewer Americans have felt connected to the political process. During the 1940s, '50s, and '60s, voter turnout regularly exceeded 60 percent of eligible voters. During the '70s and early '80s, the percentages dipped to the mid-fifties. Today presidential elections receive a 50 percent voter turnout on average. In 1996, voter turnout dropped below 50 percent for the first time in history.

Voter turnout during "off-year" (or nonpresidential) elections consistently averages approximately 35 percent of eligible voters, meaning that the fate of Congress is determined by only a third of the country. During primary elections, the number is even lower. This small band of primary voters tend to be fierce partisans and ideologically driven.

HOW TO VOTE

Although voting is a fundamental right, it is not automatic. Certain conditions to eligibility apply, such as age and being an American citizen. Persons born in the United States are automatically given American citizenship. Persons born outside of the country must take a test in order to become a citizen.

Voter Registration

Voter registration is governed by state boards of election, and is different in every state. In every state except North Dakota, citizens must register to vote before they can cast a ballot. In most states, registration must take place at least thirty days prior to the election. In some states, such as Wisconsin, registration can take place on Election Day.

Registering to vote is easy. With the passage of the 1993 National Voter Registration Act (or Motor Voter bill), citizens can register to vote as they apply for their driver's license. This has increased voter registration, particularly among young Americans. Most states' registration process requires the soon-to-be voter to select a political party (or remain independent) and provide a home address. Citizens also can register to vote at the state board of elections, post office, and at other state agencies. Registered voters are required to submit a change of address for moves within state, and reregister for moves outside of state.

Casting a Ballot

Elections are governed and run by state government. Every state has its own rules for carrying out the mechanics of voting. Most states use schools, firehouses, churches, and community centers as polling places. Registered voters are required to go to their assigned polling place, where they must show proper identification before casting a ballot. Some states have rules prohibiting candidates and their volunteers from distributing campaign literature within a certain distance from the polling places, while other states have no such restrictions.

The states also determine the hours of operation on Election Day. New York offers its voters the most time to cast their votes, opening the polls at 6 A.M. and closing at 9 P.M. Most states open the polls at 8 A.M. and close at 7 P.M. New Hampshire opens the latest at 11 A.M., while Indiana, Hawaii, and Kentucky close the earliest at 6 P.M.

Ballots come in many shapes, sizes, configurations, and levels of complexity. Some localities (most notably Palm Beach, Florida) use the now-notorious "butterfly" ballot; others use lever-booths or touchscreens; still others employ simple pen and paper.

Vote by Mail

In 1995 the state of Oregon adopted Vote by Mail (VBM) for statewide primary and general elections. Voters in Oregon had the option of either voting by mail or voting at polling places on Election Day. Since adopting VBM, voter turnout in Oregon has increased. A majority of Oregon residents now use VBM. In 2011, Washington followed Oregon's lead and mandated VBM. Colorado followed suit in 2013.

Absentee Voting

Every state allows for voters to cast their ballots from outside of the state. This is known as absentee voting, and in close elections it can sometimes make the difference in the outcome of an election.

Military personnel, college students, and business travelers most commonly use absentee ballots. The ballots can be obtained at the local board of elections. Most states require that absentee ballots be postmarked no later than Election Day.

THE EVOLUTION OF THE DEMOCRATIC PARTY

From Jefferson to Obama

At the Constitutional Convention of 1787, delegates coalesced around two general principles while writing the Constitution. The Federalists supported a strong national government, while the anti-federalists were interested in preserving the states' autonomy. Many provisions of the Constitution resulted from compromise between the two factions.

FEDERALISTS AND THE DEMOCRATIC-REPUBLICANS

Following the 1787 convention, the two factions battled over the ratification of the Constitution, with the Federalists—led by Alexander Hamilton and John Adams—winning out. Hamilton, who was appointed treasury secretary by George Washington, believed the federal government should promote a robust national economy that produced a thriving manufacturing and commercial class. In order to win passage of his programs through Congress, Hamilton cultivated and organized a group of like-minded allies to form the first political party, known as the Federalists. They recruited candidates in subsequent elections to increase their majority in Congress.

Naturally, opponents of Hamilton's policies formed their own political party. Led by James Madison and Thomas Jefferson, who was serving as Washington's secretary of state, the

Democratic-Republicans believed that the federal government lacked the constitutional authority to implement Hamilton's agenda. The Democrats, as they would eventually become known, supported an agrarian-based economy that promoted the well-being of farmers and tradesmen.

The Democratic-Republicans scored their first victory in the election of 1800, when Jefferson defeated John Adams for president. Buoyed by their success, the Democratic-Republicans began organizing at the state and local level as well, and within several years became the dominant political party. The Federalists failed to innovate or make inroads with the electorate, and in 1816 fielded its last presidential candidate, who lost in a landslide to James Monroe.

DEMOCRATS AND THE WHIGS

With the demise of the Federalists, the Democratic-Republicans came to dominate the political landscape, so much so that James Monroe's presidency would come to be known as the "era of good feeling." Intraparty squabbles, however, soon led to factions within the Democratic-Republican Party, and in the presidential election of 1824 the party fielded five candidates to succeed James Monroe. Although war hero Andrew Jackson won the popular vote, he failed to receive a majority of electors in the Electoral College. Thus, the election was thrown into the House of Representatives, where runner-up John Quincy Adams emerged victorious after striking a deal with third-place finisher Henry Clay.

Jackson's supporters were outraged by the backroom dealmaking, and splintered off to form the Democratic Party. Reviving the old Jeffersonian coalition of farmers and tradesmen, the Democrats effectively organized at the national, state, and local level, forming clubs and committees, holding rallies, establishing a chain of newspapers, and raising money for their candidates. Their rallying cry was the elimination of corruption in Washington.

Supporters of President Adams responded by cobbling together the remaining factions of the Democratic-Republican Party with remnants of the old Federalist Party. The Whigs, as they became known, lacked the Democrats' organization and were soundly defeated in 1828, 1832, and 1836. They scored their only presidential victories in 1840 and 1848 with war heroes William Henry Harrison and Zachary Taylor, respectively.

While the parties were consistent in their economic policy (the Whigs supported a national bank and tariffs that protected manufacturers; the Democrats opposed the bank and advocated low tariffs that helped farmers), both were badly split over the slavery issue. Although both tried to suppress slavery from becoming a national issue, this proved impossible as feelings and emotions intensified. Many Northern Whigs (including Abraham Lincoln) joined the newly formed Republican Party, and by 1856 the Whigs were no more.

FROM THE CIVIL WAR TO ROOSEVELT

Following the Civil War, the country's party alignment was primarily along regional lines: The Republicans held the allegiance of the Northern states, while the Democrats were strongest in those states that had formed the confederacy. This was not surprising since the

Republicans had made the abolition or limitation of slavery a key part of their political program since before the war.

The Republicans dominated national politics from 1860 to 1932, controlling Congress for most of that time and winning all but four presidential elections. During this period, the Republicans were the party that represented business interests and stood for national expansion, laissez-faire (free market) capitalism, and colonialism. By contrast, the Democrats were the party of immigrants, farmers, and tradesmen and so championed policies favorable to these constituencies.

Franklin Roosevelt's election in 1932 brought about a "realignment" of the political parties. With the Great Depression in full bloom, Democrats implemented Roosevelt's New Deal—a patchwork of federal spending programs and government regulations designed to create a social safety net for low-income Americans, particularly union workers, immigrants, minorities, and small-business owners. Between 1932 and 1980, the Democrats won seven of eleven presidential contests, and held both chambers of Congress for all but a few years.

On the Campaign Trail

As the Civil Rights Movement gained power in the South in the 1960s, aspiring presidential candidate Richard Nixon believed it was possible to detach conservative Southern Democrats from their party and make them a decisive force in electing him. He signaled in a number of speeches and position papers that he wished to limit or turn back changes made by the Civil Rights Act of 1964. This strategy, called by some in Nixon's camp the "Southern strategy," enabled Nixon to win the South and the election in 1968.

By 1972, the Democrats had largely purged their ranks of pro-segregation Southerners and were seen—exemplified in the 1972 presidential candidacy of George McGovern—as carrying the liberal standard. That has remained largely true of the party, albeit with some tacking to the center during the Clinton and Obama administrations.

THE EVOLUTION OF THE REPUBLICAN PARTY

From Lincoln to Trump

The origins of the Republican Party are bound up with the horrifying episode in American history we call the Civil War. This was the most terrible conflict in the nation's history; more than three-quarters of a million people were killed during its four-year course.

The party was founded in 1854 in opposition to the Kansas-Nebraska Act. This legislative concession to the South repealed the Missouri Compromise, an agreement by which Kansas had remained a free state in which slavery was prohibited. The party's first convention was held in Ripon, Wisconsin.

In the 1856 presidential election, the Republicans nominated John C. Fremont as their candidate. Fremont did surprisingly well, although he lost the election to the Democrats' James Buchanan. Then, in the run-up to the election of 1860, the relatively unknown Abraham Lincoln succeeded in winning the nomination of the Republican Party.

Southerners, furious at the party's antislavery stance, swore that if Lincoln were elected, they would leave the Union. When Lincoln's election in 1860 was reported, Southern states announced secession, and in a few short months the two sides were at war. Lincoln went through the war with a cabinet made up of often opposing politicians (in the words of historian Doris Kearns Goodwin, a "team of rivals") and managed by manipulation and by the strength of his personality to keep them together. He was renominated for the presidency in 1864 by a coalition of Republicans and Democratic supporters of the war, and he defeated the Democratic candidate, General George S. McClellan.

As a consequence of the North's victory in the war, the Republicans largely dominated national politics for the rest of the century. They supported a protectionist foreign economic policy and generally based their support on Eastern money and influence. (The Democrats had a more agricultural base.)

ROOSEVELT TO JOHNSON

The assassination of President William McKinley in 1901 elevated his vice president, Theodore Roosevelt, to the presidency. Roosevelt sought to break up the large business combinations, or "trusts," that had come to dominate American economic life. However, he disagreed with his successor, William Howard Taft, on a variety of issues and between them they split the Republican vote in the 1912 election, leading the Democrat Woodrow Wilson to assume the office of president.

During the 1920s, the Republican Party increasingly shifted to the right as the party of big business. This apparently winning strategy came to a crashing conclusion in 1929 with the collapse of the U.S. economy and the onset of the Great Depression. Franklin Roosevelt led the Democratic Party to victory in 1932, and although some elements of the Republican Party moved to the center and supported the New Deal, the party did not recapture the White House until Dwight Eisenhower's election in 1952.

The Republican Party's swing to the right solidified in the 1960s. In Barry Goldwater's 1964 campaign for the presidency, right-wing organizations such as the John Birch Society gained increasing influence in the upper circles of the party. Although Goldwater lost decisively to Lyndon Johnson, the drift to the right continued. In 1968, Richard Nixon's efforts to detach conservative Democrats who were appalled at their party's support for civil rights legislation resulted in his election to the presidency in 1968.

The Grand Old Party

The Republicans are often referred to as the GOP. The acronym stands for "Grand Old Party," but it has had other meanings. In 1875, when the term was first used, it stood for "Gallant Old Party." Some irreverent souls suggest that when it comes to getting voters to the polls on Election Day, the letters might stand for "Get Out and Push."

NIXON TO GEORGE W. BUSH

Nixon's immersion in the Watergate scandal injured the Republican Party, but the hurt proved temporary. In 1980, Ronald Reagan won the presidency and became one of the best-loved presidents in American history. He clothed conservative values in garments of respectability and optimism. By remaining largely detached from the day-to-day workings of his administration he was able to avoid being tainted by scandal, including the Iran-Contra scandal in which members of his government sold arms to the Iranian government in an effort to free hostages and to funnel money illegally to Central American guerilla fighters.

During the presidency of Reagan's successor, George H.W. Bush, a trend that had been in the making for some time in the party solidified: interventionism. Traditionally, Republicans had opposed foreign entanglements. This had begun to change when the party had strongly backed intervention in Vietnam. Under Bush's administration, the government forged a "coalition of the willing" to counter Iraqi dictator Saddam Hussein's invasion of Kuwait.

Such policies redounded disastrously during the administration of George W. Bush. Based on faulty intelligence of weapons of mass destruction, America invaded Iraq again, destabilizing the Middle East and inadvertently strengthening the political hand of Iran. The Bush government struggled to find an elusive victory in Iraq and, in its last year, also encountered a major financial crisis in America that saw the crash of the housing market in 2008.

THE TEA PARTY

Beginning around 2007–08, various organizations began to arise around the country calling themselves "Tea Parties." They had no unified structure and often little formal leadership, and their political agendas were diverse. But in general they agreed that America had gone off track, and they felt that the country needed smaller government, less spending, and less taxation. Many Tea Party candidates received funding from various right-wing sources, but others were largely self-financed. Although members of the Tea Party operated within the Republican Party, they were deeply critical of its leadership. Tea Party–backed candidates often challenged "establishment" Republican candidates in primary elections, and in many cases won. Within the Republican Party in Congress, a Tea Party Caucus arose.

The practical outcome of this was to push much of the Republican Party further to the right, not only on economic issues but on social issues such as same-sex marriage. Although some of the local

Tea Party groups have faded, their long-term impact is still being assessed.

The most dramatic outcome of this shift in the Republican Party was the rise of Donald Trump during the 2016 primary season. Trump's verbal attacks on immigrants, Muslims, and others played well with many in the Republican base and kept him at the front of the pack of contenders for the presidential nomination. By mid-2016, it was clear he had clinched the party's nomination as standard bearer in the election.

THIRD-PARTY CANDIDATES

An Alternative to Tradition

The two-party system distinguishes American government from most other democracies. Most Western democracies, particularly those in Europe, have multiparty elections and parliaments. By contrast, the American government traditionally has had a two-party system, and since the Civil War the two parties have been the Republicans and Democrats. From time to time, third parties have gained traction with the electorate, most recently the Reform Party, led by Ross Perot, and the Green Party. However, few third-party candidates hold elected offices at the state and national level.

WINNER TAKES ALL

Our electoral system is commonly referred to as "winner-takes-all," meaning that the candidate who receives the most votes is the one who takes office. If there are five candidates running for a Congressional seat, and candidate Jane Smith receives the highest vote total with 30 percent, she wins the election. The other finishers receive nothing.

In a winner-takes-all system, there is a strong tendency toward two parties because voters act strategically, preferring to vote for one of two legitimate contenders than to cast a "spoiler" vote for a third-party candidate. As a consequence, most voters eventually gravitate toward either the Republican or Democratic candidate.

Parliamentary systems, which are common in Europe, do not employ winner-takes-all elections. Instead, they use "proportional representation," meaning that the political parties receive legislative representation (seats in parliament) proportionate to the percentage of the vote it receives during the election. If a third party garners 5 percent of the vote, it receives 5 percent of the seats in parliament.

DUALITY OF POLITICAL ISSUES

Another reason why the two-party system thrives in American government is the duality of political issues. For the most part, there are only two sides to a given conflict. From the time of our founding (federalism versus antifederalism), to the present (pro-choice versus pro-life), most of our political debates have been two-sided affairs. It's difficult for a third point of view—and consequently a third party—to gain political traction in a two-sided debate.

That's not to say it has never occurred. At times, third parties have articulated positions and issues that have resonated with the public. What has often been the case, however, is that one of the two parties has then "co-opted" or adopted that issue as their own in an attempt to poach the third party's constituency. In the 1968 presidential election, Alabama Governor George Wallace won five Southern states by appealing to "white resentment" of minorities. Four years later, President Richard Nixon incorporated much of Wallace's message as part of his "Southern strategy," and won all five of those states. In the midterm elections of 1994, Republican challengers successfully exploited popular Reform Party issues like term limits, a balanced budget, and government accountability to end the Democrats' forty-year dominance in Congress.

THIRD PARTIES TODAY

Even though third-party members hold very few elected offices, they still play an important role in the electoral process. Voters disenchanted with the Republicans and Democrats can opt for one of several alternative parties.

Green Party

The central tenet of the Green Party is that corporations and other moneyed interests exploit average Americans for their own narrow interests, and that citizen-activists need to participate in the political process. "Greens" believe in radical social and economic reform. In the 2000 presidential election, Green Party candidate Ralph Nader garnered 2.7 percent of the national vote—the most of any third-party candidate that election—and is widely believed to have tipped the election for Republican George W. Bush in Florida, where Nader pulled crucial votes from Democrat Al Gore.

Reform Party

Founded by billionaire H. Ross Perot, the Reform Party was established in the mid-1990s to facilitate Perot's presidential ambition. At one point, the party made a serious bid to become a viable alternative to the two major parties. After Perot's second presidential campaign, however, the Reform Party lacked a coherent vision and disappeared. In 2000, it nominated right-wing political pundit Pat Buchanan as its presidential candidate. Buchanan's poor showing (he finished behind Ralph Nader in most states) combined with intraparty squabbles diminished the party, and by 2015 it had largely ceased to exist.

The only Reform Party candidate to hold statewide office was former professional wrestler Jesse "The Body" Ventura, who served one term as Minnesota's governor. Ventura pulled off one of the biggest upsets in American political history, defeating two well-known major-party candidates. Midway through his term, Ventura quit the Reform Party and declared himself an Independent.

Libertarian Party

The smallest of the three "major" third parties, Libertarians believe in radically limited government. Their organizing principle is that government should perform only two functions: protect our borders and keep civil order. Libertarian candidates tend to draw votes from disenchanted Republican voters, much the same way that Green candidates appeal to Democratic constituencies. Although it has been around the longest, the Libertarian Party is not as well organized or funded as the other third parties. Some Libertarian candidates such as Senator Rand Paul function within the Republican Party.

SELECTING CANDIDATES

Choosing Who to Run

Presidential elections are held every four years, and in most cases it's a long, contentious, and sometimes even entertaining process. Candidates spend years organizing their campaigns, and as soon as one election concludes, another one begins.

THE PROCESS

Before someone can become a major-party presidential candidate, he or she must first receive the nomination. During the winter months of each presidential year, the Democrats and Republicans hold primaries to select their respective nominees. Incumbent presidents seeking a second term rarely face a primary challenger.

The primary process officially begins with the Iowa caucus, and concludes when one candidate has accumulated enough delegates (representatives of the states) to receive his party's nomination (which usually occurs in the early spring). Once the two major parties have determined their nominee through the primary process, the general election process begins.

GETTING ORGANIZED

Running for the presidency is a massive undertaking. The candidate needs an enormous political network of supporters—contributors, volunteers, organizers, and many others. The first challenge any candidate faces when considering a run for the Oval Office is putting together a campaign organization. Serious White House aspirants begin this process within months after the conclusion of the prior election. They focus on several key tasks, including raising money, organizing the campaign network, and establishing contacts with the media.

Raising Money

Raising money—and lots of it—may be the most critical function for a presidential candidate. Seeking the White House is a wildly expensive proposition. Most experts agree that a minimum of $50 million to $100 million is required just to build an organization and be viewed as a legitimate candidate for the primary season. Another $75 million is needed to run a campaign for the general election itself. Professional fundraisers are extremely sought-after commodities. Candidates spend much of their time in the early months trying to line up proven fundraisers.

Serious presidential candidates spend the majority of their time in the months leading up to the primary season crisscrossing the country in search of campaign cash—most spend upward of eight hours a day making phone calls and attending fundraising events. Every quarter, the candidates must file a campaign contributions report with the Federal Election Commission, detailing how much money they've raised and spent. The report is available to the press, which separates the serious candidates from the "also-rans," according to how much money each raised.

Lining Up Campaign Consultants

Just as candidates compete for prominent fundraisers, they also jockey for the services of campaign consultants. Candidates look to consultants to help devise strategy, organize statewide campaigns, produce commercials, conduct polling, provide issues and opposition research, and give counsel and direction to the campaign. Political consultants with proven track records at the presidential level are difficult to come by, and are highly sought. The press looks to consultant signings as another way to separate the first-tier candidates from the long shots.

Creating State Campaigns

Because the nominating process and thus the general election are determined by state elections, candidates must have well-run campaigns at the state level. Prospective candidates put together a campaign organization in the key primary states. In states like Iowa and New Hampshire (the first two states to vote for candidates in the primary season), there is an intense competition to win the support and backing of prominent citizens including the governor, members of the state legislature, members of Congress, state party leaders, county chairmen, and even precinct leaders. It's not unusual for candidates to call and visit county chairmen, town leaders, and precinct captains directly to sign them up. Candidates rely on their state organizations to get out the vote on Election Day.

Courting the Media

During the early part of the nominating process, media attention is difficult to come by. Like everything else, candidates compete for press coverage, usually by issuing position papers, staking out bold positions, and making themselves available. National media coverage can make fundraising and organizing much easier, and elevate candidates to first-tier status.

DEBATES AND STRAW POLLS

Debates and voter forums typically begin a full year prior to the first primary. These events give voters a chance to compare the candidates, and allow the media the opportunity to assess the relative strengths and weaknesses of each candidate. More than anything, debates give the candidates a chance to gain "traction" and build momentum for their campaigns.

On the Campaign Trail

Ronald Reagan delivered one of the most memorable moments in New Hampshire primary history when he scolded the organizers of the New Hampshire primary for turning off his microphone prior to the start of the debate. "I paid for that microphone!" he retorted to the stunned moderator, setting a new tone for the campaign.

In addition to debates, the candidates also compete for momentum and perceived strength at "straw poll" conventions. These contests are usually held a month or two in advance of the primary season, and are little more than mini-conventions where citizens show up (they usually pay an entrance fee) and cast a vote for one of the candidates.

WINNING THE NOMINATION

States are free to choose how they select their political candidates. Most states use primaries to elect their political candidates; a few use caucuses. Caucuses are similar to primaries, with the big difference being that voters don't select a candidate directly. Rather, they select delegates to attend the nominating convention. Caucuses tend to have lower turnouts than do primaries, but the participants are generally more knowledgeable about the issues and tend to be more committed to their candidates.

The Iowa Caucus

The most important presidential caucus is the Iowa caucus, which is usually held during the first week in February of the election year and kicks off the formal nominating process. Presidential aspirants spend years organizing their Iowa campaign with hopes of making a strong showing.

Typically, candidates finishing among the top three in Iowa gain momentum heading into the New Hampshire primary, which takes place the following week. Candidates who fail to finish among the top three, or perform below expectations, usually begin to see their fundraising dry up and momentum stall.

The New Hampshire Primary

The primary in New Hampshire is the first in the nation, and takes place a week after the Iowa caucus. The candidates spend the week leading up to the primary traveling all over the state meeting as many voters as possible. New Hampshire voters are known for being astute and informed, and they appreciate retail politicking.

During primary season, the candidates debate one another. There has been much discussion about how these debates should be organized. Early on during the 2016 election season, the number of Republicans running for president was so large that the party was forced to separate the debates into the top-tier candidates and those with less support.

If the Iowa caucus begins the process of winnowing the field, then the New Hampshire primary concludes it. In most situations, the top two or three finishers in New Hampshire maintain enough momentum and support to continue running for president. The other finishers usually see their fundraising efforts falter and their organization dissolve as their supporters begin migrating to the more viable candidates. It is said that the top three finishers have a ticket out of New Hampshire, while the rest have a ticket home.

Because New Hampshire is such a critical contest, candidates devote hundreds of days to meeting with voters at small gatherings and events during the two-year period leading up to the primary. In no other state does this "intimate" form of campaigning take place.

Regional Primaries

After New Hampshire, the candidates who remain begin traversing the country in preparation for the South Carolina primary and Nevada caucus, and for the state contests that follow. After those contests, the candidates face off in what has been dubbed "Super Tuesday"—a day when multiple primaries and caucuses take place. The participating states devised Super Tuesday as a way to maximize their importance in the process.

Over the past decade, more and more states have begun holding their primaries earlier in the season in order to achieve greater impact on the selection process.

NOMINATING CONVENTIONS

By the end of March, the presidential nominees for both parties have been all but established. Although primary contests continue through early June, the outcome is not in doubt. Between the last contested primary and the nominating conventions, there are several weeks of "down time" during which the candidates focus on selecting a running mate, devising a general election strategy, and creating television commercials.

During these summer months, an incumbent president enjoys a big advantage. While his opponent is typically cash-strapped from the bruising primary campaigns, the president is usually flush with cash and can flood the airwaves with television commercials touting his record and attacking his opponent's. He also enjoys the advantage of incumbency, which means bill-signing ceremonies, unlimited media coverage, and the ability to set the agenda.

The political conventions take place in August and represent the formal nominating process for the two major-party candidates. In past years, the conventions offered some suspense about who would be chosen as running mates (and in some cases who would be the nominee), but today they're usually staged events with little real drama. In fact, the conventions have become so stale and devoid of news that the media networks have drastically reduced their coverage over the past decade.

ELECTION DAY

The People Decide

The general election season formally kicks off after the conventions have ended. Voters traditionally begin paying attention to the presidential contest after the Labor Day weekend, as they return from summer vacation.

TAKING A STAND ON THE ISSUES

The presidential candidates and their staffs devise a strategy for the general election that they believe will win the necessary 270 Electoral College votes required for victory. The strategies usually revolve around two central ideas: which issues should be emphasized (or de-emphasized), and how those issues should be framed. Months of polling and focus-group testing go into determining the issues and the language used to discuss them. Beginning in the late summer, both candidates use daily tracking polls in key states to detect any change in momentum.

Once they've settled on a strategy, the candidates travel to the states that they believe are necessary for victory. They attend rallies, meet with voters, and talk to the local press to get their message out. The candidate's goal is to garner media coverage while at the same time "staying on message." Given the hordes of media that follow the candidates' every move, staying on message can be difficult. A botched phrase, misspoken word, or incorrect statement can dominate the news cycle for days.

The candidates typically "contrast" their records and philosophy with their opponent's, pointing out the strengths in their candidacy and the weakness in their opponent's. As Election Day draws near, this type of negative campaigning usually intensifies—especially if the contest is close. During the waning days of the campaign, it is not unusual for a candidate to drop an "October surprise"—a particularly nasty revelation—about his opponent with the hopes of gaining an advantage.

Media Coverage

Media coverage intensifies as the general election begins in earnest following the nominating conventions. Dozens of reporters travel with both candidates, reporting on their every move, utterance, gesture, and campaign squabble. With information closely guarded by the campaigns, reporters are often left to report on the machinations of the campaigns rather than the candidates themselves.

On the Campaign Trail

Heading into the presidential debates, both campaigns play the "expectations game" as they try to convince the media that the other candidate is expected to perform much better. In 2000, the Bush campaign masterfully lowered expectations for their candidate, so much so that when Al Gore failed to deliver a knockout blow during the first debate, it was considered a Bush victory.

The general election debates are the only unguarded—some would say unscripted—moments of the campaign, where the candidates are left to their own devices. The presidential candidates participate in two debates, which are televised on all the major networks.

For the candidate who is trailing, the debates represent the best opportunity to change the dynamics of the race.

Election Day

Election Day takes place on the Tuesday after the first Monday in November. In the days leading up to Election Day, the presidential candidates zigzag across the country, visiting key states to make a last appeal to voters.

The media—most notably the television networks—typically try to forecast (or call) the results as soon as the polls have closed. Even though it takes hours for the actual results to come in, they make these predictions based on "tracking polls" that are performed throughout the day. Tracking polls are simply polls that are conducted of voters as they leave the polling place. These polls aren't always accurate, because people often misrepresent their actual vote when speaking to the media. The media combines tracking-poll information with historical voting data to predict results, sometimes with alarming inaccuracy. In 2000, it was the breakdown of this statistical modeling that twice led to incorrect calls in the Florida race.

THE ELECTORAL COLLEGE

The president and vice president are actually elected by the Electoral College. When casting a ballot for a particular candidate, voters are actually voting for a slate of electors. These electors in turn will vote for that candidate in the Electoral College.

The Electoral College system was devised for two reasons: The framers of the Constitution had feared direct democracy (they believed that a college of dispassionate citizens were better suited than the masses to select a president), and they wanted to protect the interests of smaller states and rural areas.

The Electoral College is composed of 538 members—equivalent to 100 senators, 435 House members, and three representatives from the District of Columbia. Each state's number of electors equals their number of representatives and senators. Thus, California has the most electors with 55, followed by Texas (38), New York (29), Florida (29), Pennsylvania (20), and Illinois (20). The Electoral College is a winner-take-all system, meaning whoever carries the state—regardless of the margin—receives all of the state's Electoral College votes.

Calls to Reform

Following the 2000 election, there was some discussion about eliminating the Electoral College and replacing it with direct voting. Were that to happen, however, chances are the candidates would focus on large population centers such as New York, California, Florida, and Texas, and ignore the interests of rural and sparsely populated areas.

In 1977, President Jimmy Carter proposed a constitutional amendment that would do just that, but the amendment failed to win a two-thirds majority in the Senate. Small-state senators had also rebuffed a measure to eliminate the Electoral College in 1969. The major parties oppose eliminating the Electoral College because it would give more influence to third-party candidates, who under the current system stand almost no chance of winning any electoral votes.

Who Are the Electors?

It's important to keep in mind that the candidates choose their own slate of electors—the Republican candidate has his set of electors, and the Democrat candidate has a different set of electors. State rules determine how these electors are chosen. The Constitution does not require that the electors cast their ballots for their pledged candidate in the Electoral College. However, since the candidates themselves choose their slate of electors, it's extremely unlikely that any elector would vote for someone other than his pledged candidate.

THE MEDIA AND GOVERNMENT

The Fourth Estate

Outside of government institutions, no other entity has more influence in shaping policy decisions and elections than does the mass media. Although the framers of the Constitution could never have envisioned the proliferation of mass media that we enjoy today, they were acutely aware that the press would play a critical role in the burgeoning democracy.

AN EMERGING INFLUENCE

The media's role in government dates back to the colonial era, when daily newspapers were the primary source of news for the colonists. Newspaper publishing was an expensive and time-consuming process at that time. The fastest of printing presses could only produce 250 newspapers an hour. The reporting of "breaking" news took a matter of weeks, not days. Sometimes it took months for information to travel throughout the colonies.

Around the time of the American Revolution, twenty-five weekly newspapers served the colonies. Some were vocal supporters of the cause of independence, while others adamantly opposed it. Just about all of them lost money, because publishing costs far exceeded the demand for daily papers.

It wasn't long after the creation of political parties that the Federalists and antifederalists began publishing their own newspapers. These papers were little more than crude party organs that advocated the party platform, promoted their candidates, and relentlessly attacked the opposition. These party-affiliated papers had small audiences, and relied heavily on their respective parties for financial support.

The Transformation of the Media

The mass media has undergone an incremental transformation over the past 200 years. Transformative changes began in the mid-1990s with the advent of the Internet and all-news cable television channels. As those and other communication technologies continue to evolve, seemingly at lightning speed, the role of the media in government will also continue to change.

The Golden Era of Newspapers

With the advent of the steam-powered printing press in the 1830s, the situation began to change. Able to produce a greater number of newspapers at a cheaper cost, newspaper publishers began to forgo support from the political parties—and stopped advancing their partisan causes—in order to attract larger audiences.

The intense competition for mass readership led to a rapid expansion in the number of daily newspapers and in their circulation. Between 1870 and 1900, newspaper circulation grew from 3 million to 15 million—a 600 percent increase.

The period of 1880 to 1925 is considered the golden era of newspapers, as daily papers wielded enormous influence with politicians, business leaders, and the public. Publishers and editors used this power to influence public opinion, shape policy decisions, and highlight social injustices.

Radio and Television

In 1920 the Westinghouse Electric Corporation's KDKA in Pittsburgh became the nation's first commercial radio station, but it took a decade for the new medium to catch on with the public. By 1930, however, almost 40 percent of the households in America owned radios, and that number would double again before the end of the decade. President Roosevelt helped to popularize the new medium during the Great Depression with his weekly "fireside chats." With its ability to deliver breaking news instantly, radio replaced newspapers as the primary source of news for most Americans.

Television enjoyed an even faster rise to prominence. In 1939, fewer than 5 percent of the households in America owned a television. In 1950, that number had grown to 90 percent. One survey revealed that by the mid-1960s, a majority of Americans received their news information from television. As the Vietnam War dragged on, Americans increasingly turned to television for a "firsthand" account of the war. Coverage of other big events, including President Kennedy's assassination, Watergate, and the Apollo 13 crisis, also helped cement television's primacy as the predominant source of news and information in America.

The Impact of the Internet

Websites such as Drudgereport.com, Breitbart.com, Huffingtonpost.com, and many others receive millions of hits a months from visitors seeking news, information, and opinions that aren't found in the mainstream media.

In 1998, it was controversial cyber journalist (some would call him cyber gossip columnist) Matt Drudge who broke the Monica Lewinsky scandal. Drudge didn't do the firsthand reporting on the story; he simply revealed that the magazine *Newsweek* had the story but was undecided about publishing it. Drudge's revelation forced *Newsweek* to print the story, setting off a chain of events that ultimately led to President Clinton's impeachment. Since then, dozens of political stories have originated in cyberspace, only to cross over to the "mainstream" media.

The Internet has been an invaluable tool for journalists to perform research, gather information, and report from distant parts of the globe. It has allowed the media to be more comprehensive and timely in its reporting, and has effectively reduced the news cycle from twelve hours to a matter of minutes.

THE ROLE OF MEDIA IN GOVERNMENT

In a democracy, the free flow of information, ideas, and opinions is critical. To this end, the media has three primary responsibilities: setting the agenda, investigating the institutions of government, and facilitating the exchange of ideas and opinions.

Setting the Agenda

Every day, hundreds of decisions, activities, and events take place in Congress, the executive branch, and the courts that could potentially have an impact upon millions of Americans. It's the job of the media—print, television, radio, and the Internet—to determine which actions merit coverage and which do not. This is part of the news-gathering process. After all, print and broadcast media have a finite amount of time and space to dedicate to news coverage.

The process of determining the news—setting the agenda—is not a perfect science. What one editor considers "hard news" might not be viewed as newsworthy at all by another. It's a highly subjective process that leaves many news-gathering organizations open to criticism from groups dissatisfied with their coverage. For years, political conservatives have complained that "elite" media institutions such as the *New York Times*, *Washington Post*, and the broadcast networks (ABC, NBC, and CBS) were biased toward liberal causes (the exception being Fox, which is largely conservative).

Investigating the Institutions of Government

As we have learned, the framers of the Constitution established multiple checks and balances to guard against tyranny. Their biggest fear was that one branch of government would monopolize power and rule against the will of the people. One of the checks they established is the First Amendment, which guarantees a free press.

In this regard, the media serves as a kind of "super-check" on all three branches of government. For more than two centuries, the press has called attention to corruption, deception, incompetence, fraud, abuse, and the misuse of power at every level and branch of government. For example, it was a vigilant press that brought attention to unsanitary working conditions in factories and the misuse of child labor around the turn of the twentieth century, and uncovered government deception and lying during the Vietnam War. Perhaps most famously, it was Bob Woodward and Carl Bernstein, two novice *Washington Post* reporters, who conducted an investigation of the Watergate burglary that led to the resignation of Richard Nixon.

With the proliferation of cable television, talk radio, and the Internet, the media is more active than ever in serving as a public watchdog. Entire publications, news programs, and websites are dedicated to exposing government malfeasance, corruption, and waste.

The Rise of the Muckrakers

Investigative journalism dates back to the 1800s, when a new breed of reporters dubbed "muckrakers" sought to expose public corruption and social injustices. Many of them, including Ida Tarbell, Lincoln Steffens, and Ray Stannard Baker, were associated with *McClure's* magazine.

Facilitating the Exchange of Ideas and Opinions

Every day, tens of millions of Americans listen to talk-radio personalities such as Rush Limbaugh, Sean Hannity, Michael Savage, Bill O'Reilly, and others to get their perspective on the day's news and events. Audiences do not listen to these programs to receive objective information or dispassionate analysis; quite the opposite, they usually share the host's political point of view.

Serious lawmakers and opinion leaders use the Sunday morning shows to influence the debate, shape policy, and make headlines. A strong appearance on one of these programs can sometimes change the discourse surrounding a political issue, and catapult a personality to national prominence.

INFLUENCING THE MEDIA

Elected officials, nonelected government workers, and political candidates spend a considerable amount of time figuring out ways to shape media coverage. The following five techniques are commonly used:

1. *Staged events.* The most common (and reliable) way to attract media coverage is by staging an event. In 1994, the House

Republicans had a "signing ceremony" on the Capitol steps to launch their "Contract with America" campaign theme. The event received enormous press coverage.

2. *Off-the-record conversations.* Politicians, bureaucrats, and candidates have off-the-record conversations with reporters when they want to disseminate certain information, but don't want that information associated with them. Reporters usually attribute off-the-record comments to anonymous or unnamed sources.

3. *Sound bites.* Most elected officials are adept at giving "sound bites" (concise and colorful quotes) to reporters. Officials who consistently deliver the best sound bites usually receive the most coverage.

4. *Trial balloons.* From time to time government officials will float "trial balloons"—anonymous program or policy ideas—to the press in order to gauge the public's reaction. Trial balloons allow officials to test ideas or potential appointments without taking responsibility for them.

5. *Leaks.* Almost every day in Washington, confidential information is passed from government officials to the media. Leakers typically do this for one of two reasons: to cast a negative light on their opponents, or to strengthen their point of view on a particular matter among their colleagues or constituents.

THE FUNCTION OF MEDIA IN POLITICAL CAMPAIGNS

The media exercises its greatest influence during elections. Every aspect of a political campaign, from fundraising and press announcements to staged events and major speeches, is planned with an eye toward garnering media coverage. Political candidates need television, newspapers, radio, magazines, and the Internet to reach voters with their message. Candidates who lack an effective media strategy are likely to be destined for failure.

Political Advertising

The vast majority of media coverage during political campaigns comes in the form of paid political advertising. With the cost of television advertising skyrocketing, candidates are forced to spend an inordinate amount of time at fundraising to pay for it.

Candidates routinely spend 80 percent of their "war chests" on television and radio advertising. In larger states such as California, Texas, and New York, television advertising is the only way for candidates to reach the tens of millions of voters.

Most television advertising comes in the form of thirty-second commercials. Increasingly, the trend has been toward negative advertising (or "contrast" ads, as political pros refer to them), mostly because they have proven to be highly effective—even though voters claim to be turned off by them.

Spinning the News

All candidates supplement their paid media with free (or earned) media. Free media is another way of saying news coverage, and it's invaluable in establishing the reputation and credibility of a candidate. Lawmakers and candidates can shape the news coverage in several ways. The most obvious is by planning campaign events at photogenic or interesting backdrops (known as photo-ops)—something that President Reagan's handlers mastered.

Astute politicians also develop close relationships with particular reporters by granting them exclusive interviews, sharing campaign information, and coming up with fresh campaign stories on a daily basis. All of these are things that make reporters' jobs easier. And of course, all candidates and their staff are adept at "spinning" the news, a process by which they try to convince reporters that their interpretation of the news is the correct one. "Spin doctor" is a derisive term used to describe campaign staffers whose sole responsibility is to spin the media.

On the Campaign Trail

During the 2016 presidential campaign, Donald Trump garnered huge press coverage by saying outrageous things about immigrants, Muslims, and other groups. Other Republican candidates complained that the media was focusing so much attention on Trump that he was "sucking the air out of the room" for the rest of them.

THE MEDIA AND THE PRESIDENCY

Hundreds of "beat reporters"—journalists who cover the White House on a daily basis—work from the basement of the White House. Twice a day, these reporters meet with the president's press secretary to get a briefing on the day's activities. Television cameras covering these briefings have been a frequent source of friction between the press secretary and the press, as some journalists use these press briefings as an opportunity to grandstand for the cameras. Typically, the press is on call twenty-four hours a day, unless the press secretary puts a "lid" on the news, which means that no big announcements are planned.

Most presidents have "feuded" with particular journalists and publications at one time or another. Richard Nixon detested the *Washington*

Post and *New York Times*, and had his vice president publicly attack them. The Clinton White House singled out Sue Schmidt of the *Washington Post* as a reporter with a vendetta against the president. President George W. Bush publicly used an expletive to describe *New York Times* reporter Adam Clymer, a sentiment that Vice President Cheney agreed with. President Kennedy, on the other hand, enjoyed a cordial relationship with the press corps, partly because he singled out favorites for special treatment in return for favorable coverage.

In spite of the tension between the president and the press corps, the two have a symbiotic relationship. The president needs the press to deliver his message, and the press needs access to the president in order to do its job. It's not uncommon for White House staffers to leak information to select journalists in order to shape the coverage. Sometimes the president will grant exclusive interviews to certain reporters as a way to dominate the headlines.

Pool Reporting

The reporters who cover the White House beat form a tight-knit fraternity. When the president travels abroad or makes domestic appearances, only a limited number of reporters can travel with him. When this occurs, the reporters adopt "pool coverage," which means that the reporters attending the event share their notes with the "pool"—the reporters not in attendance. Some beat, or specialized, reporters collaborate with their colleagues from other news outlets to make certain that they haven't missed any details or facts from a presidential event.

MONEY, PORK, AND INFLUENCE

Greasing the Wheels of Government

In 1834, the French chronicler Alexis de Tocqueville remarked that America was a nation of joiners. That observation still holds true today. Americans love to form and join groups. Our country is replete with all kinds of associations, clubs, organizations, societies, and fraternities of every conceivable variety. There are more than 200,000 associations in the United States, and it is estimated that two-thirds of all Americans belong to at least one. While not every one of these organizations is politically active, the fact remains that through the years interest groups have come to play an important role in American government.

WHAT ARE INTEREST GROUPS?

Interest groups are associations or organizations of individuals who share a common interest and assert their collective strength in the political process to protect—and in some cases expand—that interest. These groups may form for many reasons: to celebrate a common heritage, pursue a political or social agenda, shape a policy debate, or strengthen a profession or avocation. Some interest groups, such as the National Association for the Advancement of Colored People (NAACP), are well known; others, like the National Anti-Vivisection Society, are obscure.

Often, mass social movements such as the fight for racial equality or the effort to outlaw alcohol consumption spawn the formation of interest groups. It's not unusual for countergroups to appear in response. For instance, Putting People First (PPF), a 35,000-person organization, mobilized to counteract the efforts of People for the Ethical Treatment of Animals (PETA).

Every year, thousands of interest groups are formed, each with its own distinct purpose and agenda. With the proliferation of communication technologies such as the Internet and mobile phones, it's easier than ever for individuals to form groups, communicate with each other, and act in unison.

HISTORICALLY SPEAKING

Lobbyists have been around since the beginning of America's history. Various groups attempted to influence Parliament and then, after American independence, groups sought to influence or control members of Congress. This process reached new heights in the late nineteenth century. Lobbyists during what was known as the Gilded Age began to develop an unflattering reputation with the public and in the press. Poet Walt Whitman referred to them as "crawling serpentine men, born freedom sellers of the earth." In 1869, *The Nation* magazine, one of the country's most influential and respected journals, described a lobbyist as "a man whom everybody suspects; who is generally during one half of the year without honest means of livelihood; and whose employment by those who have bills before a legislature is only resorted to as a disagreeable necessity."

Some good did come from special interest lobbying during this time, however. Pressure from various activist organizations and associations brought about much-needed electoral reforms, child labor and wages-and-hours laws, antitrust and business regulations, a federal income tax, and women's suffrage, among other things.

Perhaps the most successful interest group from that era was the Anti-Saloon League, the driving force behind the adoption of the Eighteenth Amendment, which from 1919 until its repeal in 1933 banned the sale of alcohol in the United States. The group left nothing to chance during its twenty-year quest to outlaw alcohol consumption, publishing monthly newsletters, staging rallies at the Capitol, forming local temperance groups, organizing letter-writing campaigns, making political contributions to friendly lawmakers, and targeting hostile members of Congress who lived in districts where the citizens favored prohibition.

On the Campaign Trail

For some time the National Rifle Association (NRA) has exercised a huge influence on American politicians. During the 2012 election cycle, 261 candidates received contributions from the NRA.

TYPES OF INTEREST GROUPS

Interest groups vary greatly in their missions and memberships. Some are dedicated to a single issue; others represent professional organizations and associations; still others are advocates for the "public interest." Their size can range from millions of members to several dozen. Some wield enormous clout while others have limited influence. Most interest groups can be classified into three categories: economic, public-interest, and single-issue.

Economic Interest Groups

The primary purpose of a vast majority of interest groups is to provide economic benefits to their respective memberships. Business groups, labor organizations, and professional associations are examples of interest groups that seek to gain economic advantages.

One of the most influential business groups is the U.S. Chamber of Commerce. Representing more than 200,000 companies nationwide, the chamber's lobbying expenses exceeded $64 million in 2015. The chamber lobbies on behalf of its members for laws and regulations that promote economic growth and commercial activity. The National Association of Manufacturers is another powerful business lobby. Its sole focus is to support legislation that creates manufacturing jobs and oppose bills that eliminate them.

Labor unions are another type of business interest group. The American Federation of Labor and Congress of Industrial Organizations (AFL-CIO) ranks among the most powerful interest groups, with more than 13 million members. Every year it contributes millions of dollars to political candidates and provides grassroots campaign support at the local, state, and national level. The overwhelming majority of its campaign contributions and assistance is given to Democratic incumbents and their Democratic challengers. The Teamsters and the United Auto Workers (UAW) are also powerful labor lobbies, with 1.5 million and 800,000 members respectively.

Professional associations compose another type of economic interest group. The American Medical Association (AMA), Screen Actors Guild (SAG), and American Bar Association (ABA) are three of the most influential professional associations in America. During the 2000 election, the AMA contributed several million dollars to candidates, making it one of the largest political contributors in

America. The Screen Actors Guild often uses the star power of its membership to lobby Congress and the White House for favorable treatment.

Public-Interest Groups

A fairly recent category of interest groups is the so-called public-interest group. The mission of public-interest groups is to protect the rights, resources, and liberties common to all Americans—in other words, to act "in the public interest."

The American Civil Liberties Union (ACLU) is known primarily for its involvement in legal battles related to the abuse of civil liberties. The ACLU is also a forceful lobby on Capitol Hill against legislation that impedes the Bill of Rights, particularly the First Amendment.

The modern public-interest movement traces it origins to the 1960s, when citizen-activist Ralph Nader created a consumer watchdog group called Public Citizen. Over the past four decades, Nader has formed or sponsored more than fifty public-interest groups, including Citizen Works, The Health Research Group, and the Public Interest Research Groups (PIRG), an activist organization funded and controlled by college students.

Common Cause, another grassroots public-interest group, played an important role in winning passage of the Twenty-Sixth Amendment (which extended the right to vote to eighteen-year-olds), the Government in the Sunshine laws of the mid-1970s, and campaign finance reform. It works on nonlegislative issues as well, such as achieving greater voter registration.

Environmental organizations such as Greenpeace, the Environmental Defense Fund, the Sierra Club, and the National Wildlife

Federation (NWF) are considered public-interest groups. Greenpeace takes a more radical approach to fulfilling its vision, while the Sierra Club, NWF, and others work within the political system to achieve policies that protect the environment. The Nature Conservancy uses contributions from its members to purchase and preserve undeveloped open spaces.

Single-Issue Groups

Some of the most prominent and powerful interest groups in America are "single-issue" groups. These organizations have one thing in common: an extremely narrow and intense focus on a particular issue. The abortion debate, for example, has created single-issue groups on both sides of the argument. The sole focus of the National Abortion Rights Action League (NARAL) is to keep abortion legal; the National Right to Life Committee (NRLC) would like to see abortion outlawed. Both camps aggressively advocate their positions on Capitol Hill, in state capitols, and through the media.

THE LOBBYISTS

The K Street Connection

Since the very first Congress, interest groups have played an important role in shaping legislation. They have used an assortment of methods to influence legislators and impact public policy. These tactics can be divided into two categories: direct and indirect techniques.

DIRECT TECHNIQUES

Lobbying policymakers directly is the preferred method of influencing the process. Many interest groups hire specialized lobbying firms or retain lobbyists on their staff to help gain access to key decision-makers. With their vast network of contacts and intricate knowledge of the political process, former legislators and staff members typically make the best lobbyists.

Lobbyists perform a variety of functions to shape government policy:

- Set up private meetings with lawmakers, staff, and executive agency bureaucrats to inform them of their clients' interest
- Provide both policy and political information to decision-makers
- Assist lawmakers and their staffs in drafting legislation
- Testify before Congressional committees, subcommittees, and executive rule-making agencies on proposed legislation and rules related to their industry
- Interpret the impact of proposed legislation and rules

- Organize protest demonstrations
- Host campaign fundraisers for candidates
- Talk to the media
- Run advertisements in the media
- File lawsuits or engage in other litigation

Most interest groups aren't shy about offering campaign assistance to lawmakers in order to gain access and shape policy. The larger interest groups have special fundraising committees called political action committees (PACs), which distribute campaign contributions to various federal and state lawmakers. Interest groups give PAC donations to incumbents and challengers who they believe are sympathetic to their cause. Since the late 1970s, the number of PACs has quadrupled to nearly 5,000, with the size of their contributions increasing tenfold to $500 million. Labor PACs give most of their dollars to Democratic candidates, while corporate donations tend to favor the Republicans.

A few prominent interest groups, such as the Americans for Democratic Action (ADA), the American Conservative Union (ACU), and the League of Conservation Voters (LCV), publish an annual "scorecard" whereby they rate the performance of every member of Congress. For example, if a lawmaker has an ACU rating of 80, it means that he voted in favor of the ACU's position 80 percent of the time on legislation that the group deemed important. Members with a high ACU rating usually have a low ADA rating, and vice versa.

INDIRECT TECHNIQUES

Sometimes, interest groups will work through third parties to influence legislators and shape public policy. One of the most commonly used indirect techniques is constituent lobbying, whereby members of an organization write, phone, and e-mail legislators to communicate their concerns. When done correctly, this type of grassroots lobbying can be extremely effective because it demonstrates the size, intensity, and political savvy of an interest group—something elected officials monitor closely. Members of Congress pay particularly close attention to correspondence from constituents who are responsible for maintaining and creating jobs in the lawmakers' districts or states.

The Creation of Super PACs

One result of the Supreme Court's *Citizens United* decision was to allow the creation of super PACs. These organizations are prohibited from making any direct contributions to candidates or parties, but they are permitted virtually unlimited independent spending in support of or against issues and candidates. The effect of super PACs has been to vastly increase the amount of money spent in political campaigns.

In some cases, well-funded and high-profile interest groups try to generate a groundswell of public pressure through mass mailings, public demonstrations, media advertising, and public relations campaigns. In 1993, the Health Insurance Association of America, a group opposed to Hillary Clinton's nationalized healthcare proposal, spent $17 million on a series of television commercials to discredit the first lady's plan. The ads were highly effective in turning public opinion against "Hillary-Care." And the National Association for the Advancement of Colored People (NAACP) used protests, boycotts, and other forms of civil disobedience to persuade lawmakers to pass the landmark Civil Rights Act of 1964.

On extremely high-profile matters of public policy, like-minded interest groups sometime band together to influence public opinion. In their effort to defeat the passage of the North American Free Trade Agreement (NAFTA), dozens of consumer, environmental, labor, and manufacturing groups formed an "umbrella" organization called the Citizens Trade Campaign. By pooling their resources, the groups were able to reduce expenses, avoid duplicating each others' efforts, and give the appearance of broad-based support.

REGULATING LOBBYISTS

Although it tried on several occasions, it wasn't until 1946 that Congress finally passed the first law regulating lobbying activity—the Federal Regulation of Lobbying Act. This law, however, only pertained to Congressional lobbying; it did not regulate lobbying of the executive branch or federal agencies.

The primary purpose of the act was to provide public disclosure of lobbying activities. It required lobbyists (defined as any person or organization that was paid to influence Congress) to register with the clerk of the House of Representatives or the secretary of the Senate, state their purpose for lobbying, and provide quarterly updates on their clients and fees.

The law quickly proved to be ineffective, however, as lobbyists exploited several loopholes to avoid compliance. It was further weakened by a 1954 Supreme Court decision that held that the act only applied to paid lobbyists, groups, or organizations whose principle purpose was influencing Congress, and lobbyists who contacted members of Congress directly. Individuals who lobbied Congressional staff, were unpaid, or who performed other services in addition to lobbying did not have to register with Congress. As a consequence, fewer than seven thousand individuals and organizations registered as lobbyists, even though ten times that number were believed to be engaged in lobbying activities.

On June 11, 1995, at a public event in Manchester, New Hampshire, President Clinton and House Speaker Newt Gingrich shook hands on a promise to pass campaign finance and lobbying reform. While the former pledge was forgotten, the latter was acted upon, as the two parties came together to pass the Lobbying Disclosure Act of 1995. The law overhauled the 1946 act with six new provisions:

1. It defined a lobbyist as anyone who spent more than 20 percent of his or her time lobbying members of Congress, their staff, or executive branch officials.
2. It banned for life former U.S. trade representatives and their staffs from lobbying for foreign interests.
3. It banned nonprofit groups that lobby Congress from receiving federal grants.
4. It required lobbyists to file semiannual reports disclosing the specific issues and bills worked on, the amount of money spent, and the branches of government contacted.
5. It required lawyers who represent foreign entities or U.S.-owned divisions of foreign-owned companies to register with Congress.
6. It exempted grassroots lobbying efforts and lobbyists who are paid less than $5,000 semiannually.

The law had an immediate impact, as the number of registered lobbyists doubled almost immediately. It also revealed the size and scope of the lobbying activities of foreign governments in Washington.

INFLUENCES OVER FOREIGN POLICY

Just as domestic policy is influenced by interest group pressure, so too is foreign policy. While foreign governments are prohibited from lobbying the institutions of government, scores of ethnic-American organizations regularly lobby Congress and the president on behalf of their countries of concern. The American Israel Public Affairs Committee (AIPAC) was rated by *Fortune* magazine as the fourth most powerful lobbying group in Washington. With a staff of 150 and an annual budget of $15 million, it has considerable clout on Capitol Hill.

STATE GOVERNMENT

"All Politics Is Local"

In our system of government (federalism), the federal and state governments share power. Under federalism, the functions of government are divided. The federal government has exclusive domain over international affairs and national defense. Other matters, such as education, crime control, housing, and taxes, fall within the province of both the federal and state governments. There is a healthy tension between the federal and state governments over the roles and responsibilities of each.

FEDERAL VERSUS STATE

State government is structured similarly to the federal government, except on a much smaller scale. Every state has a constitution and three branches of government—executive, legislative, and judicial. The states also have a power-sharing relationship with their local and municipal governments that's much the same as the federal system.

The states are often referred to as the "laboratories of democracy," because no two state governments are exactly alike. Often policies, laws, and procedures that are successful in one state are copied in another, and then in the federal government. This tendency to adopt the "best practices" of states has kept state government vibrant and innovative.

STATE CONSTITUTIONS

Every state has a constitution that establishes the legal and political framework for government within that state. Some state constitutions are well written, while others are not. None captures the flexibility, durability, and sheer brilliance of the Constitution of the United States. Most are wordy, bulky, disjointed documents that have been amended, revised, and rewritten many times. Alabama has the lengthiest constitution at a mind-numbing 172,000 words—about twenty-five times longer than the U.S. Constitution! Vermont has the shortest at fewer than 7,000 words.

State Constitutions and the Federal Constitution

State constitutions are "subordinate" to the supreme law of the land, meaning that provisions of state constitutions that come into conflict with federal law are considered unconstitutional. However, state constitutions are the supreme law of the state for matters that fall outside of federal law or that aren't expressly prohibited by the Constitution of the United States.

Like the U.S. Constitution, state constitutions enumerate the powers of the three branches of government, create state agencies, establish a bill of rights, and provide for a method to amend the constitution. Beyond that, state constitutions tend to be very detailed (some would say maddeningly so) about certain matters. For instance, the California constitution mandates the size of fruit boxes, while the Louisiana constitution dedicates nearly 5,000 words (almost the entire length of the U.S Constitution) to the creation of the board of commissioners of the port of New Orleans. That same Louisiana constitution also proclaims former Governor Huey P. Long's birthday a "legal holiday forever."

In many states, extremely narrow provisions, like Alabama's cap on local tax rates, have forced lawmakers to repeatedly amend the constitution as government has grown in size and complexity. Some constitutions have provisions idiosyncratic to their state, such as Oklahoma's requirement that all public schools teach horticulture, stock-feeding, and agriculture.

THE POWERS OF THE GOVERNOR

Running the States

The governor is the highest elected state official and the most powerful officeholder in the state. Gubernatorial authority is confined to state matters only; a governor does not have any federal powers. Historically, the statehouse has been a wonderful launching pad for national office—twenty-three governors have gone on to serve as president or vice president.

A BRIEF HISTORY

During the colonial era, governors were appointed by the king of England. The position was considered largely symbolic, because governors were vested with little real power. The elected state legislatures distrusted their governors' ties to the king, and as a result the legislatures and the governors rarely cooperated on anything. Following the Declaration of Independence, the initial state constitutions called for appointed (not elected) governors to serve one-year terms, which left the governors virtually powerless.

After the U.S. Constitution was ratified in 1789, states began rewriting their constitutions to reflect a stronger executive branch. Governorship became an elected position (most states adopted two- and four-year terms) with enumerated powers. Just about every state modeled the new position after the presidency, and as the nation grew more comfortable with executive power at the national level, so too did it begin to accept the governors.

Throughout the nineteenth century, state governors began to assume more and greater powers. By the end of the nineteenth century, governors were some of the most influential officeholders in the country. They lorded over their political parties, controlled statewide patronage positions, administered state funds, wrote state budgets, and convened special sessions of the legislature. To this day, the governors remain at the epicenter of the political process across the states.

On the Campaign Trail

The 2016 presidential race featured two governors—Louisiana's Bobby Jindal and New Jersey's Chris Christie—running for the GOP nomination. Both suspended their campaigns before the end of the nomination process; Christie endorsed the campaign of Donald Trump.

The statehouse is by far the most popular route to the presidency. Four of the last six presidents—George W. Bush, Bill Clinton, Ronald Reagan, and Jimmy Carter—were governors. Governors tend to make good presidential candidates because they have a wealth of executive experience, understand how to delegate authority and responsibility, and can point to a specific record of accomplishments and successes. Moreover, they usually remain untainted by the partisanship and "Inside the Beltway" bickering that bedevil senators and congresspersons who seek national office.

GUBERNATORIAL POWERS

As the chief executive of his or her state, the governor has many responsibilities and duties. Like the president, he has enumerated, constitutional, and symbolic powers. Some states are said to have strong governors, meaning that the office holds many enumerated powers. The strongest governor of the nation is the governor of New Jersey, who has the ability to appoint cabinet positions (including the state attorney general) as well as state supreme court justices. Conversely, the Texas governor has almost no constitutional powers, and is considered the weakest of the fifty governors. The governor's powers can be divided into three primary categories: executive, legislative, and leadership.

Executive Powers

In most states, the greater part of the governor's authority stems from the executive powers outlined in the state constitution. This includes everything from declaring a state of emergency (due to natural disaster, civil unrest, or other unforeseen situations) to calling up the National Guard. Just as the president is the commander in chief of the U.S. military, the governor is the commander in chief of his state's National Guard. Following the terrorist attacks of September 11, 2001, many governors called up the National Guard to help protect their airports, ports, and other public areas.

The governor's most important role as chief executive is drafting an annual state budget. At the beginning of each year, the governor submits a budget to the state legislature that outlines spending and policy priorities for the year, as well as any tax hikes or cuts. The governor and the state legislature then negotiate back and forth on spending levels and programs until the two branches reach a compromise. Many states, including New York, California, and New Jersey, have mandatory deadlines for when a budget must be passed. If the governor and the leadership of the state legislature are from the same party, meeting this deadline is rarely a problem. During times of divided government, however, the process can become acrimonious and protracted. In New York, the budget deadline is rarely met.

Legislative Role

Like the president, the governor also has the ability to influence and shape the legislative process. As the highest elected statewide officeholder, the governor can be viewed as a representative of the entire state. As such, most governors—particularly during their first term in office—propose ambitious legislative agendas. Governors will typically travel around the state and meet with community groups, business leaders, and local officials in order to drum up support for their agendas.

Once a year, the governor lays out his or her agenda in the State of the State address, a speech given before a joint session of the legislature. Like the president's State of the Union address, the State of the State is the one opportunity for the governor to provide a vision and a cohesive plan for the future. In every state except North Carolina, the governor has the ability to veto legislation passed by the state legislature. Just like the presidential veto, the threat of a gubernatorial veto is sometimes more powerful than the veto itself.

Leadership

Part of the governor's power is derived from his or her ability to lead. No other state officeholder can attract national media attention, influence national lawmakers, galvanize the public, and shape the national party like the governor.

Some governors use the "bully pulpit" of the statehouse to build support for unpopular or controversial policies. In 2000, Illinois Republican Governor George Ryan put a moratorium on all death-row executions after it was learned that a few convictions were tainted by questionable evidence. The move initially angered many voters, but after intense public lobbying he was applauded for the decision.

STATE LEGISLATURES

Doing the People's Business

Every state has a state legislature, which works with its respective governor in creating laws and setting public policy. Many similarities exist between Congress and the state legislatures: They both represent and serve their constituents, work with executive leaders to pass laws, stand for election every two and four years, and receive their power from the state constitution.

The power, prestige, and influence of state legislatures vary from state to state. In weak-governor states, legislatures have a greater impact on policy formation and decision-making than they do in strong-governor states. One thing that is consistent throughout the fifty states is the location of the state legislature; each meets at the statehouse, which is located in the state capital.

WHO SERVES IN STATE LEGISLATURES

Most state legislative positions are part-time jobs with low-paying salaries. Not surprisingly, New York and California pay the best, topping out at more than $90,000 for their upper chamber positions. Alabama occupies the bottom, paying out a mere $10 stipend per legislator for every day in session.

Most state legislatures are in session for only several months a year. The legislators spend the rest of the time providing constituent casework services in their districts. This irregular schedule, combined with the low pay, typically leads to a high turnover rate in most state legislatures. Most states have an age restriction on serving in the state legislature, with the average minimum age being twenty-one.

Generally speaking, there are two broad categories of citizens who serve as state legislators. The first are career politicians with upwardly mobile career ambitions. Many congresspersons, senators, and governors learn their trade in the state legislature, and use it as a launching pad to the national level. The second group is composed of civic-minded citizens with long-standing and deep ties to the community. These members share a passion about issues that might seem mundane to others—helmet laws for skateboarders, the size of parking spaces for the handicapped, hunting season dates, and so on.

SIZE AND ORGANIZATION

State legislatures vary greatly in size. New Hampshire has more than 400 legislators representing only 1 million residents, while New Jersey has 120 legislators representing more than 6 million citizens. Nevada has only 60 state representatives for its population of 1.5 million.

Bicameral or Unicameral?

With one exception, every state has a bicameral (two-chamber) legislature. The exception is Nebraska with its unicameral (one-chamber) legislature. Most states refer to their upper chamber as the State Senate, and their lower chamber as House of Representatives, House of Delegates, State Assembly, or General Assembly.

The leadership in the state legislatures is similar to that of Congress, with a Speaker and majority and minority leaders in the lower chamber, and a senate president and major and minority leaders in the upper chamber. Chamber leaders tend to be even more powerful than Congressional leaders because party discipline is stricter at the state level.

POWERS AND AUTHORITY

The process of passing legislation in the state legislatures is similar to that of Congress, although the subject matter can differ greatly. State legislatures take up everything from new state holidays to the medical use of marijuana, gay marriage, assisted suicide, highway speed limits, ban on cell phone usage in cars, and much more. There are five areas in particular where state legislatures focus most of their attention: education, roads and highways, health and welfare benefits, law enforcement, and conservation.

Education

Anywhere from a quarter to a third of most state budgets are allocated to the education system. A majority of the money goes to the state colleges and universities. Tuition for schools such as Rutgers University, the University of Michigan, the University of California at Berkeley, and the University of Texas is much lower than that of comparable private schools because of state subsidies. (At state universities, out-of-state students typically pay more tuition than do in-state students.) In recent years, state universities have been forced to raise tuition for in-state students because of state budget cuts.

While local municipalities are responsible for administering primary and secondary schools, the state legislature sets the education guidelines, such as the number of days in a school year, graduation requirements, statewide testing, teacher licensing, and so on.

Roads and Highways

Most states allocate approximately 10 percent of their annual budgets for the construction and maintenance of roads and highways. This includes constructing highways, filling potholes, removing snow, establishing speed limits, mandating seat belt usage, and licensing drivers. For many state legislators, the Department of Motor Vehicles is an unending source of complaints from their constituents.

Health and Welfare Benefits

It's not uncommon for state legislatures to allocate a quarter of the state budget to health and welfare benefits for the sick and unemployed. State agencies administer state hospitals, immunization programs, welfare benefits, unemployment insurance, and scores of other programs aimed at helping needy citizens. They also regulate medical professionals, as well as private hospitals, nursing homes, and other care centers.

Law Enforcement

While local government is primarily responsible for maintaining law and order, every state has its own police system. State police departments are typically responsible for enforcing civility outside of major cities and towns, and for maintaining highway safety.

Conservation Efforts

State legislatures play an important role in conserving public lands, establishing state parks, and regulating hunting and fishing. State legislatures can conserve lands by allocating funds to purchase them, or by simply "protecting" them (this is usually done to protect endangered animals or ecosystems).

COUNTY GOVERNMENT

The Step Below the State Level

County government is the most common jurisdiction of local government throughout the United States. Every state but three—Alaska, Rhode Island, and Connecticut—is composed of county governments of varying size and population. Although Rhode Island and Connecticut are geographically divided into counties, they do not have county governments. (Connecticut abolished them in 1960.) Alaska refers to counties as "boroughs," because they do not want to stigmatize them as tools of state government; in Louisiana they are called parishes. Loving County, Texas, is the least populous county with only 82 residents as of the 2010 census, while Los Angeles County is the most populous—it's home to 9.8 million people, as of the 2010 census. In total, there are 3,066 counties in the United States, each with its own local government.

Counties trace their origins to England, and they are modeled after the English shire of the Middle Ages. Back then, each shire was an administrative arm of the national government, as well as the province of local government. Early American colonists adopted the shire as they settled the Eastern Seaboard.

Until World War II, county government was little more than a resource for states to administer the services of government. However, with the dramatic growth of suburbs beginning in the 1950s, the role of county government began to change. Over the past several decades, counties have assumed more responsibility and power from the states, and have begun to provide greater services to their residents. Today, county governments are important providers and administrators of critical government services.

BASIC FUNCTIONS

County governments are unique in that, unlike cities, they are not incorporated, and unlike states, they have no reserved or constitutional powers. By and large, the primary task of county government is to administer the functions delegated to them by the state. This includes maintaining rural roads and highways, reassessing property values, keeping official records, providing food and welfare assistance, constructing and maintaining county buildings, awarding county contracts, and collecting taxes. In effect, a county government serves as a middleman between local and state government. For many residents of rural areas, county government provides a crucial link to the larger world.

Growth of County Government

Over the past two decades, the demands and expectations of county government have grown more substantial. Functions that were historically completed at the state and federal level are now the responsibility of county government. Following the terrorist attacks of September 11, 2001, for example, county police and fire departments have played a larger role in maintaining homeland security.

TYPES OF COUNTY GOVERNMENT

A vast majority of county governments take one of three forms: commission, commission-administrator, and council-executive. In all three forms of government, county commission members receive little or no pay (these are part-time positions) and serve a term of four years. It's not uncommon for county commissioners to seek higher office at both the state and national level.

Commission Government

Sometimes referred to as "board of commissioners" or "board of supervisors," the commission is by far the most common form of county government. Two-thirds of the counties in the United States have a commission that contains three to five commission members. In a commission government, the elected board acts as both the legislative and executive branches. It has the power to adopt budgets, enact regulations, set policy direction, and appoint county officials. Most county commissions are composed of elected officials; some are composed of judges, town supervisors, and city officials.

Commission-Administrator Government

In a commission-administrator system, the commission board appoints an administrator who serves at the board's discretion. In some counties, the administrator is nothing more than a symbolic figure with little power. In other counties, the administrator has a wide range of responsibilities and duties, such as appointing department heads, drafting a budget, overseeing construction projects, and promulgating regulations.

Council-Executive Government

Under this system, a county executive is elected by the county at large, and serves as the chief administrator. The county executive typically has the power to hire and fire department heads, formulate a budget, set policy direction, and veto legislation passed by the county council or commission. The primary difference between the commission-administrator and council-executive forms of government is the separation of powers principle—the elected county executive is totally independent from the council or commission.

Other County Officials

In addition to a county executive and county legislators, most counties have four other important elected positions:

1. *County clerk.* The county clerk is responsible for keeping the official records of the county, such as birth and death certificates, mortgages, deeds, and adoption papers, as well as issuing marriage, automobile, and business licenses. The county clerk also oversees elections, and is usually elected to a four-year term.

2. *Sheriff.* The county sheriff is responsible for providing law enforcement to areas of the county that are not incorporated towns. Most county sheriffs oversee the county prison, and are responsible for enforcing court dates. The county sheriff's authority varies from county to county. Some are elected; others are appointed.

3. *County attorney.* Sometimes called the district attorney, prosecutor, or the state's attorney, the county attorney is the legal advocate for the county in all civil lawsuits brought against it. The county attorney also conducts criminal investigations and prosecutes lawbreakers.

4. *County assessor.* The county assessor has one of the most important jobs of local government: He or she is responsible for determining the value of residences within the county for tax purposes. The county assessor periodically performs revaluations of all properties throughout the county to ensure that there is a consistent and fair tax basis, but does not assess new taxes.

CITY AND TOWN GOVERNMENT

Democracy in Action

When the United States was founded, it was composed of rural communities and dispersed towns. With the exception of New York, Philadelphia, and Boston, very few cities existed. More than 90 percent of the population was farmers. Today, just the opposite is the case. Almost 80 percent of the population lives in or near a metropolis (a city with at least 50,000 residents).

Some states define cities as any town or municipality (regardless of size), while other states regard large municipalities as cities, and smaller ones as boroughs, towns, or villages. Unlike counties, which are created by the state, cities are formed when a group of citizens come together and write a charter.

CITY CHARTERS

For a city to be officially recognized, it must be incorporated; to be incorporated, it must first have a charter. A city charter is similar to a state constitution—it outlines the power and structure of the government, including elections and appointments. There are four types of city charters:

1. *Home rule*. The home rule is the most popular form of incorporation. It allows residents to draft a city charter, which is then put before voters for approval. Voters must also approve any amendments to the city charter. Home rule charters can be granted by the state constitution or the state legislature. When

granted by the state constitution, a home rule charter must be in accordance with the provisions of the constitution—when the two are in conflict, the state constitution wins out. When granted by the state legislature, a home rule charter is subject to revocation at any time by the state legislature.

2. *General charter.* Under the general charter, cities are classified according to population size. This system allows for the similar treatment of both large and small cities. The general charter is the second most common form of incorporation after home rule.

3. *Optional charter.* With an optional charter, citizens can vote on one of several charters allowed by the state. It gives residents a direct voice in the incorporation process, and allows them to shape their government. Optional charters are becoming increasingly popular.

4. *Special charter.* The special charter is the oldest form of incorporation still in use, although it has fallen out of favor in recent years. Special charters are extremely time-consuming because their provisions are specific to each new city. For every new city, there must be a new charter. Moreover, any amendments to a special charter must be passed by the state legislature—an extremely cumbersome process. It's doubtful that special charters will remain in use much longer.

On the Campaign Trail

Chicago was, for many years, openly run on political patronage, administered by Mayor Richard J. Daley. The system was openly corrupt, offering jobs in exchange for an agreement to get out the vote for the Democratic Party machine.

CITY GOVERNMENT

Once a city is incorporated, it must choose a form of government. Cities have several options to choose from: mayor-council system, council-manager system, and commission system.

Mayor-Council System

Also known as the strong mayor government, the mayor-council system is the most common form of city government. In this system, both the mayor and a unicameral city council are elected. The city council is composed of either districts or at-large members. In most situations, the mayor has the authority to veto legislation passed by the city council, hire and fire city administrators and department heads, and draft a budget.

Council-Manager System

Sometimes referred to as the weak mayor form of government, the council-manager system was a reformist innovation devised during the Progressive Era of the 1910s. Under this model, the city manager is a nonpolitical administrator responsible for running the daily operations of the city. He or she is usually appointed by the city council and provides little leadership outside of his or her prescribed duties. Even if the mayor is elected, the mayorship is largely a figurehead title. Consequently, the weak mayor system is popular in smaller cities. This form of government has been rejected by larger cities, because of their need for experienced political leaders and decisive action.

Commission System

This is the least common of the three systems—only about 100 cities nationwide use a commission. Under this scenario, an elected board of commissioners performs the operations of the city and oversees the departments and agencies. A mayor is sometimes chosen from the commissioners, though it's a largely ceremonial position. The commission system has been criticized for its lack of a single authority and reliance upon consensus. Commission systems are popular in reform-minded states. Spokane, Washington; Des Moines, Iowa; and Birmingham, Alabama, are three of the best-known commission cities. In 1960, Galveston, Texas—the birthplace of the commission system—abandoned it for a weak mayor system.

NEW ENGLAND TOWN GOVERNMENT

In Massachusetts, Vermont, Rhode Island, New Hampshire, and Maine, a different system of government is used: the New England town hall. In this region of the country, towns consist of one or more incorporated villages and the surrounding countryside.

The New England town meeting is a form of direct democracy in which all the citizens participate equally in decision-making and governance. An annual town meeting is held. At this meeting, the voters decide on a budget, taxes, school expenditures, and other annual matters. They also elect a school board, tax collector, and road commissions, as well as a five-person "board of advisers" that manages the town on a day-to-day basis.

In some of the larger towns, direct democracy of this nature is too unwieldy and difficult. In such cases, the townspeople elect delegates to represent them at the town meeting. Increasingly, these towns are beginning to adopt weak mayor or modified council-manager plans in order to keep up with population growth and the growing complexity of governance.

SPECIAL DISTRICTS

Government entities known as special districts carry out some municipal and county government functions. Special districts are established by state law, and are typically governed by elected boards with the help of professional staff. Special districts are single-purpose governments, meaning that their sole function is to perform one task, such as fire prevention, sewage treatment, rural irrigation, or pest control. The distinguishing characteristic of a special district is its power to impose taxes and borrow money to finance its services, as well as spend federal funds. The property tax is the most common type of levy for special districts. It is believed that California employs the most special districts, estimated to be in the tens of thousands.

School Districts

By far the most common type of special district is the school district. In 1812, New York City created the first school district to determine where students should attend school. At one point in time, there were more than 100,000 school districts in the United States. After several decades of consolidation, that number has been reduced to about 15,000.

School districts are particularly common in states where the cities or counties do not administer the school systems (this occurs in about half the states). Although they come in varying sizes, school districts everywhere have one thing in common: They are run by an elected or appointed board. This board appoints a superintendent to administer the school system, and makes broad policy decisions for the district. The board also determines the district's curriculum, creates school boundaries, and makes decisions about building new schools. Board decisions are usually well publicized and highly scrutinized by district residents.

School district elections are some of the most hotly contested political contests at the state and local level. Ambitious public servants frequently use school board positions as entry points into the political system, and many school board members go on to serve in city and state government.

REGIONAL GOVERNMENT

Over the past several decades, the idea of "regional government" has gained popularity in cities and towns across the United States. Regional governments are government entities that extend beyond city or town borders, but fall short of county government. For example, the city of Indianapolis formed a regional government when it merged with most of its neighboring suburbs. Both Nashville, Tennessee, and Miami, Florida, have formed similar regional governments with their neighboring communities.

Regional governments are attractive to city planners and politicians because they allow communities to combine resources and spend tax dollars more efficiently. Dozens of entities can be classified as regional governments, though only a few are commonly used:

- *City-county consolidations.* Some cities have merged with the outlying county to form a regional government. New York City and New York County serve as one governmental entity, as do Miami and Dade County, Florida. City-county consolidations are most common in large metropolitan areas.
- *Federations and voluntary associations.* These types of associations are commonly used to coordinate transportation planning in rural areas. For example, four counties in Indiana formed the

Northeastern Indiana Regional Coordinating Council to provide transportation planning for the region.

- *Regional councils.* Perhaps the most popular form of regional government is the voluntary regional council. The National Association of Regional Councils estimates that there are more than 450 regional councils in the United States, and it defines them as "multipurpose, multi-jurisdictional, public organizations created by local governments to respond to federal and state programs."

- *City mergers.* It's not unusual for cities to merge with or annex neighboring cities in order to create a more powerful regional authority. In some states, annexation is difficult and acrimonious. In other states, such as Texas, annexation is more common and straightforward. Several noteworthy cities—San Diego, Tampa, Atlanta, Houston, and Phoenix—have annexed neighboring communities as part of their growth strategy.

- *Sale of services.* Many local governments contract with larger cities (and even counties) to provide basic services of government, such as police, water, sanitation, fire protection, and street maintenance. This type of arrangement is considered a regional government because it involves the shared planning of resources. Many small communities would not be able to develop were it not for this type of regional government.

- *Single purpose entities.* The Metropolitan Atlanta Rapid Transit Authority (MARTA) is also a regional government. But perhaps the most well-known single purpose entity is the Port Authority of New York and New Jersey. Its mission statement is to "identify and meet the critical transportation infrastructure needs of the bi-state region's businesses, residents, and visitors." It was created in 1921 to settle harbor boundary disputes between the two states.

LOCAL POLITICS

Local government serves as a basic starting point for citizens who want to enter the political process. Some citizens seek local office out of a commitment to public service. Others have a specific agenda in mind, such as rolling back property taxes, changing zoning ordinances, reassessing property values, renovating public landmarks, and so on. And still others use local government as a stepping stone to higher political office. In fact, many local leaders combine all three motives.

Local government provides a good entrance into the political process for several reasons. First, the cost of campaigning is relatively modest compared to higher office; the biggest expenditure is usually printing fliers and running local radio ads. Second, local office is rarely a full-time job, which makes campaigning less rigorous and stressful than it is for higher office. And third, candidates start off with a base of support—friends, neighbors, former high-school classmates, business associates, and acquaintances. It is difficult to seek higher office without a foundation of support.

Local government officials can best be described as citizen-politicians—most work full-time jobs during the day and focus on local government at night and on the weekends. One of the strengths of our system of government is that the process is open to everyone, not just professional politicians and career public servants. The Founding Fathers intended for our government to be the province of citizen-legislators, and at the local level this remains the case.

INDEX

Constitution. *See also* Amendments to
Constitution; Bill of Rights; Congress;
Executive branch; House of Representatives;
Judicial branch; United States Senate
  bicameral legislature and, 20–21
  cabinet and, 121–22
  case law and, 156–60
  case law expanding meaning of,
    156–60
  contents (articles) overview, 24–31
  key doctrines defining federal model,
    29–30
  presidential succession, 96–97, 115–17
  ratifying, 20–23
  state constitutions and, 33, 140,
    229–30
  writing and compromising, 19–21
Constitutions, state, 33, 140, 229–30
Council-executive government, 242–43
County government, 240–43
Courts. *See* Judicial branch

Declaration of Independence, 12–15
Democratic Party, evolution of, 180–84
DHS (Department of Homeland Security),
  174–75
Districts, special, 248–49
Due process, 35

Education system, 124, 238–39, 248–49
Electoral system. *See also* Political parties;
  Presidential elections
  Electoral College, 203–5
  electors, 205
  general election, 201–3
  "winner-take-all" approach, 190–91
Executive branch. *See also* President;
  Presidential elections
  checks and balances, 160–61
  duties and limitations, 28
  establishment of, 27–28

FBI (Federal Bureau of Investigation), 171–72
The Federalist Papers, 22–23, 121
Federalists, 22–23, 34, 108, 180–81, 206–7
Filibusters, 62
First lady, 109–11
Foreign policy, influencing, 227

Governors, 231–35
  becoming president, 232
  history of, 231–32
  leadership role, 234–35
  legislative role of, 234
  powers of, 233–34
Green Party, 192
Gun ownership, 40–41

Hamilton, Alexander, 22–23, 88, 113, 121,
  180–81
Harrison, William Henry, 59, 96, 182
Health and welfare benefits, 239
Homeland security (DHS), 174–75
House of Representatives. *See also* Congress;
  Interest groups and lobbyists; Laws,
  making; United States Senate
  about: overview of, 46–47; term limits,
    46–47
  bicameral legislature and, 20–21
  caucuses and cliques, 53
  committees, 49–52
  creation of, 24–25
  eligibility requirements, 54
  leadership positions, 47–49, 51–52
  rules, 52–53
  Senate vs., 71

Immigration matters, 156
Impeachment, 25–26, 28, 29, 60, 99,
  107–8, 116, 209
Interest groups and lobbyists
  about: overview of, 216, 222
  economic interest groups, 219–20